SELF-LOVE, SELF-HEALING

Using the Mind and Body to Get Unstuck, Heal Old Wounds, and Live Abundantly

Christina Nylese

Self-Love, Self-Healing

Copyright © 2025 Thought Leader Academy Publishing

Cover design by Claudine Mansour Design. Interior design by Michael Beas.

Published by Thought Leader Academy Publishing

3901 North Kildare Ave

Chicago, IL | 60641

ISBN: 979-8-9922572-6-7

Author's Note

Don't underestimate the significance of your pain.

It's your pain.

It's real, and it matters.

And I see you.

I'm here to show you that there is a way out.

Love,

Your Hope Dealer

Dedication

We are not meant to be on this journey alone.

To my mom, who continues to remind me that the most important moment is the moment we are in.

To my dad in heaven, who was my guiding light throughout this process. You always knew I'd do it.

Contents

Introduction

I began writing this book for those who, like I once did, feel broken and helpless in the grip of alcoholism. My goal was to inspire others to have hope with my journey of surrender and resilience. Having found my path to healing—one that extended beyond the 12-step recovery program—I wanted to share that experience with those seeking a similar transformation.

But as I wrote, the book took an unexpected turn. I came to realize that I was never truly broken—and none of us are. We may be fractured, but we are not beyond repair. Some say that hope is a negative word because it indicates striving for something we don't have. I disagree. Hope was the first feeling I can remember holding onto for dear life, and it was hope that kept me from giving up.

For so long, I saw myself as a victim in my own story, unaware that another way to live even existed. But I found a way out—a path to freedom. Each chapter reveals more of that journey, from my teenage obsession with perfection to battling a full-blown eating disorder in my twenties and eventually struggling through destructive alcoholism until I found sobriety at age thirty-nine.

Through telling my stories here, I realized I'm anything but a victim—and I didn't want to write from that perspective. We all face challenges but also possess the power to overcome them. This book is about healing and finding inner peace, a reminder that we have the strength within our minds and bodies to mend our fractures and move through life's difficulties.

It became clear that God had different plans for the message I was meant to share. I've come to understand that believing in something greater than myself is the key to freedom. When my thoughts align with that greater source, they have the power to change the trajectory of my life.

In this book, you'll learn about the three most powerful tools I discovered on my path back to wellness, using my mind and body, that not only healed me and still do but offered me a transformation from hopeless to abundant:

1. Mindset and Mindfulness

2. Nourishment

3. Connection

You'll also be guided on how to create an abundant life using these tools when we explore how to reclaim time to experience more time freedom. I'll walk you through the step-by-step process I use consistently to turn my time into an asset that works for me instead of me working for it. My unique process will reinforce to you that you are the CEO of your own life and health.

My path to healing leads to one destination—a place ripe with opportunities. It is the path to living abundantly, in health, wealth, peace, and happiness. I want this and more for you, and I am beyond thrilled to be your guide on your journey.

Let's get started!

I'm Christina, and I'm an Alcoholic

"You can choose to be a victim to your circumstances or take responsibility for how you choose to perceive them." — Jen Sincero

The last year of my drinking, in 2010, I confined myself to my bedroom with a bottle of vodka and *Days of Our Lives*. The only emotions I could feel were rage at everyone and everything for thinking they had all the answers regarding my well-being. I was in such denial that even after everything I had been through, I still would not admit that I had a problem with alcohol. I had already been to jail three times for driving under the influence, in and out of rehab centers, fired from jobs, and bankrupt. I lived for the opportunity to sneak out on my bike to go to the closest liquor store that I hadn't been to yet that week to get my bottle of vodka with the money I stole from my mom's hidden stash. But I didn't think I had a problem.

My mom watched me like a hawk, suspicious of my every move. She had to lock up her booze in the garage closet because, undoubtedly, I'd drink it and then fill the bottle with water to make it look like I didn't. She never came into my room, so I stashed empty bottles of vodka all over my bedroom and waited for the opportunity to bring them over to the country club and throw them in the garbage can by the tennis courts. But just in case she did decide to come into my room in the middle of the night when I was sleeping, I always kept a stash of vodka underneath my mattress or my pillow. Plus, I knew it would be there when I woke up because I could hardly get out of bed unless I had some alcohol in my system. The tremors were too rough.

I felt trapped because I was in no condition to work, nor did I have any motivation to pull myself together to go find a job. I was drunk 24/7 at this point, so living with my mom was my only option. Getting sober and getting my shit together was barely a consideration. And my family thought that my drinking was about willpower. They didn't understand the nature of the disease any better than I did. They thought all I needed to do was not drink, and everything would magically fix itself as if it were as easy as deciding what to eat for dinner.

It was easier to hide in the comfort of my room with my cat, Linkin, and only come out when my mom had left for the day. She played golf in the mornings, so I'd wait until I heard her pull out of the garage to stumble into the kitchen and make coffee. I was too afraid she'd notice my hangover even though I knew that she knew. I just didn't want to experience shame and humiliation over and over again. Then, I'd make my way to the liquor store. Golf took four hours, so I had plenty of time. By the time she came home, I was at least feeling physically better, having quelled the shakes with more booze. Sometimes, I was completely wasted, and other times, I was able to keep my composure.

The longer this went on, the sicker I became emotionally, spiritually, and physically. I didn't eat. I just drank. I was malnourished and depleted of energy. My brain was failing me, and I felt dumb. As the year progressed and the physical compulsion of the disease became worse, there was no denying that I was sick. I knew that there was help out there. I knew that the rooms of recovery existed, but I couldn't bring myself to go. I don't know if it was pride, or if I thought that someday I would drink like a normal person again, but I could not bring myself to admit that I could no longer drink and needed to do something about it. I felt sorry for myself, and to numb the feelings of shame, guilt, self-loathing, and resentment, I just drank more. The level of my drinking became so dangerous that I would go to bed at night and pray to God that I didn't die in my sleep if I hadn't already passed out.

This isn't happening to me; it's happening for me.

It wasn't until years later, after getting sober, that I could say that with conviction.

What finally happened was nothing short of divine intervention. I had enough human interventions that didn't work, but I truly believe that God stepped in to say *enough is enough! I need you here to do my work.* Not everybody survives this disease called Alcoholism, so not one day goes by today that I don't thank God that I'm still here.

Here's what happened.

On May 25, 2011, the day I had my last drink, I rode my bike over to my friend's house, and she noticed I was drunk. She didn't confront me about it but acted as if everything was normal. When she offered to drive me home with my bike in the back of her SUV, she drove me directly to a detox center instead. The detox center could not admit me right away, so she drove me back to my mom's, and it was agreed that I would pack my suitcase and go to the detox that night for intake. You may think, "That's not divine intervention! That's human manipulation!" Interventions can look a bit like trickery, but when someone you care about has their life on the line, you do what you think is the right thing. I like to think of it as human intervention led by the divine.

The funny thing is, I wasn't even mad at my friend. I was grateful. I felt relieved, as though the fight was over. By the end of the day, the alcohol wore off, and I actually shared a meal with my mom before she drove me back to the detox center. I assumed I was coming home after my five days there, so I was relaxed and looking forward to being somewhere safe where I couldn't drink. By this time, I knew I needed help.

After five days, I did not go back home to my mom's house. In fact, when I asked the nurses if my mom was picking me up, they told me that she had called to leave me a message. "Drink or don't drink. I don't care anymore. But you will never come back here to live again."

I was in shock. I was not prepared for this. I had a suitcase of clothes, no money, no credit cards, and no car. My mind was racing, trying to think about what I was going to do and where I was going to go. It was the first time I felt completely alone and abandoned. It felt as if I had no options. Except, there was one option, so I had the nurse drive me to my brother's house.

I slept on my brother's couch for almost a week before I was able to get a bed in the local homeless shelter. It was either that or live in the woods. "Just do this for Mom," he said. That was my attitude at first: to appease her, and then maybe she would let me come back home. But once I got to the shelter, something changed inside of me. I had the most miraculous shift emotionally and spiritually that I had ever experienced before.

It was June by the time a bed was available. I hadn't drunk alcohol since May 25th, nor had I even thought about it. I sat by the front desk in the lobby to check in at the shelter. There were doors, but I couldn't see what was on the other side of them. The attendee at the desk paid no attention to me while I waited. I felt scared sitting there all alone. As I looked around the room, I thought to myself, "*Look at where you are! What are doing? You can do so much better than this! You know this about yourself!*" And right there, after ten years of denial and uncontrollable drinking, I surrendered. For the first time in forever, I felt excited anticipation. I felt hope. I felt relieved.

You may be thinking, *was it really that easy?*

The thing about surrender is that when it happens, it's swift. It happens instantly when you reach your personal worst bottom, and in that moment of clarity, which is nothing short of miraculous, you have a choice. I'd had bottoms where I could make a choice before, but I missed the opportunity because I was in so much denial. This time, there was no denying my plight. My choice was to continue drinking and die, or stop drinking and live a better life. At that moment, my future life flashed before me. I could see all the things I hadn't yet done, the experiences I was yet to have. As far as I was concerned, the only way from where I was standing was up, so I chose life, surrendered, and never looked back.

My humility brought me to my knees and gave me the strength to let go of many things while living at the shelter, namely my reliance on other people to survive. Relying on others to survive day-to-day is very different from asking for help. Relying on others to survive means waiting around, expecting them to clean up your mess. Asking for help is rising to the occasion and taking responsibility for yourself.

The shelter was small. There was a common area outside where people smoked cigarettes. Dorm rooms accommodated around 25 people who shared three showers and two sinks. The bunk beds cost $7 a week. On my first night there, a nice lady gave me some tea tree oil in a plastic spray bottle with some lotion and water to spray down my bed before going to sleep. She told me bedbugs didn't like tea tree oil. I'm not even sure if that's true, but I was grateful to her because I never caught sight of a bedbug, nor did I wake up covered with bites.

I was allowed two drawers but I only needed one since the only thing I had was my cell phone and a knapsack with a few changes of clothes. Upon my arrival, I was given a chore to help in the kitchen and serve the other residents dinner. Again, I was grateful to have this particular chore when I could have been scrubbing toilets or mopping floors. The worst part was wearing silly hairnets, like the kind they wear in the deli of your grocery store. I never thought twice when I saw it on someone else, but I felt a little self-conscious at first when I was wearing it. I made friends in the kitchen quickly. The chef became a good friend, and I am still friends with him today. We were lucky to have him. He was also there trying to stay clean and out of trouble and blessed us each night with the culinary skills he'd used throughout his career at five-star hotels and restaurants around the world. He always made me something special if I asked for it. Again, I was grateful for the people coming into my life, the healing powers of being of service, and learning to show up and be responsible again.

Coffee was served at 5:00 a.m. each morning, and if I wanted a cup, I had to get up and be in line by 4:45 a.m. I learned to get up by 4:30 a.m., splash my face with water, and throw on a baseball hat so I could get my morning fix. Whoever had coffee duty did a really good job. I was thrilled to find that they offered a variety of creamers in different flavors. *Wow, what an unexpected surprise!* I was again grateful I could have a great-tasting cup every single morning. The little things made me truly happy at this point.

I would sit by myself in the little room with the TV and read my daily inspirational journal. It became a ritual, and I looked forward to it every day. I did not mind getting up early. There was something extremely peaceful about that time of day. Most of the residents didn't bother getting up that early, so I had space to myself. I found myself enjoying going to bed at night sober and waking up without a hangover, just in time for a sunrise with a clear head and clean conscience.

It didn't take long for me to notice that I felt the happiest I had been in a very long time. I was free from my family's scrutiny, the daily guilt and shame of drinking, and wasting my life away. As scared as I was to move into the shelter, I was safe and lucky to have a bed to sleep in. I watched people come in and out daily from county jail or from living in the woods. They'd come in for a few days just to get a shower and a good meal, and then they'd be back in the woods, living in their tents. I'd see them walking their bikes during the day with all their belongings in grocery bags. Over time, they'd collect so many things, and I just didn't understand how they had the stamina to transport everything from one place to the next. I always wondered: do they even know where they're going? Do they have a destination in mind?

I was very aware I had an opportunity to start over. Life was simple and uncomplicated for the time, which was exactly what I needed to get myself back on my feet. I was doing this without the ultimatums from family, friends, or the law. I was able to take responsibility for myself and finally stop acting like the way my life turned out was everyone else's fault. I was finally doing this for me.

"Today, I will refuse to think, talk, speak, or act like a victim. Instead, I will joyfully claim responsibility for myself and focus on what's good and right in my life." — Melody Beattie

\When I surrendered to my disease, I found hope, humility, and gratitude again. The power of all three gave me the momentum to keep pushing forward and helped me free myself from feeling stuck.

Arriving at the shelter felt like the end of a war for me. The battle inside my mind, my body, and my soul came to an abrupt end. It was like taking the deepest breath I had ever taken while letting go of all of the resistance, all of the pain, and all of the self-loathing all at once. I would be lying if I said it was easy, but it was extremely liberating. I did not have all the answers. I did not know what was best for me. There were others who came before me who had experienced my pain and got to the other side. I was finally willing to let both them and God lead.

I've been an addict of some kind my entire life. By twelve, I was a perfectionist; by seventeen, I struggled with an eating disorder. In my thirties, I struggled with alcohol, and in my forties, I found myself addicted to a man. It felt like a never-ending cycle—just as I overcame one addiction, another would take its place. Much of my life was spent unaware of the unresolved trauma fueling these patterns, causing my addictions to continually resurface in different ways.

I never spent too much time living in the past to unravel things in order to create a healthy and prosperous future. It deserves some observation and consideration, which I did while writing this book. In hindsight, I can clearly see where my destructive and self-sabotaging thinking and behaviors came from. With this awareness, my healing continues to evolve by focusing on the present moment, living in gratitude, and focusing on what is good in life more than focusing on what's wrong with it. When I was drinking, 98% of my time was spent dwelling on everything that was wrong with my life. I kept myself stuck there, so no wonder I couldn't move forward.

I'll talk a bit about our negative self-talk, which I call the bully voice, because it's something that, for many of us, has been a part of our life since we were young and continues to beat us down into adulthood. Practicing mindfulness has been one of the most powerful healing modalities I've used, which I will explore in length with you here.

Mindfulness, which is simply how we pay attention to the present moment, is the only way that I know of to cultivate awareness. And without awareness, we cannot change. I will walk you through my experiences with this after getting sober in 2011. For me, it was a jumping-off point, and from there, with the awareness, a new version of myself was born.

IDENTIFY

Chapter 1: Start With Why

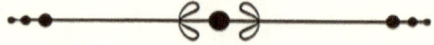

A Why Statement is intentional. It's bold. It's transformative.

Before we dive in, I invite you to create space in your mind and heart for the changes you want to make in your life. Maybe you are looking for a physical health transformation or a life with less chaos and more peace, but you don't know where to start. Perhaps you just need some inspiration and motivation to live your life differently. You may be curious about how to heal your emotional pain with a more holistic and natural approach.

In any of these cases, there is a specific reason you are reading this book. Take a few minutes to reflect and ask yourself *Why*. Keep in mind that over time, your *Why* will change. As we grow in health, we seek new ways to expand as we continue the transformation process.

Someone recently asked me what the most significant health event in my life has been. For me, that was an easy answer. Getting sober was the most significant because, without it, I would have had no health journey at all. When I chose to get sober, my *Why* was that I didn't want to die. Of course, I wanted to create a better life, but I was afraid alcohol would kill me.

After ten years of very destructive drinking and a few near-death experiences, I not only reclaimed my physical health but experienced a profound spiritual and mindset shift that altered my future path. From there, my passion for helping others to heal from addictions grew into a health coaching practice that uses natural solutions and the power of our minds and bodies to get to the other side.

How to Use This Book

This book is divided into five parts: *Identify*, *Mindset and Mindfulness*, *Nourishing Habits*, *Connection*, and *Create the Life You Want*. Throughout each, I share my challenges with multiple addictions to give you insight and a different perspective as you transition from feeling stuck to gaining a sense of freedom. We are all faced with adversity at some point in our lives. It is part of the human experience. It's never easy, and some can navigate through it more easily than others. I learned how to use the power of mind, body, and spirit to heal, and I continue to use these self-healing tools to rise to new levels in my life.

Whether it is transformation or just interest in how to use the power of your mind and body to get unstuck, I invite you to read the book in its entirety and then revisit the chapters that resonate with you the most. The stories within don't follow a chronological timeline, as I chose to write in the order I now use in my coaching programs—we start with our mindset, then we explore how to nourish ourselves from the inside out; we embrace the power of connections with others, self, and spirit, and lastly, we create the life we want by using our time intentionally and opening ourselves to opportunities of abundance everywhere.

I've included Self-Healing Invitations so you can get into action right away because we have all learned by now that information does not equate to transformation. My hope for you is that you will be inspired to act in whatever way feels right to you so that you can align yourself with the abundance of life that is available to you today.

You can find all of my Self-Healing Invitations, recorded meditations and essential oil education on my resource page by scanning this QR code. I have provided this QR code throughout the book after each Self-Healing Invitation for easy access as well.

Self-Healing Invitation: Why Statement

Let's declare our *Why*. Start by reflecting back to when you bought this book:

When I saw this book, I felt:

I bought this book because I want to or am curious about:

My top three health and wellness concerns are:

I have already tried to address these concerns by:

I am excited to learn how to:

Now, take a moment and be still. Take a deep breath in and a long exhale out. Rub your palms together to generate some heat and place them over your heart to open your heart chakra.

Now ask yourself these questions:

Who am I showing up as right now?

How do I want to show up for myself and others?

How do I want to feel?

I only have one life. How do I want to live it? What does that look like?

What energy do I need to embody in order to achieve that?

Next, write down three things you desire with regard to your physical, emotional, or spiritual well-being:

1.

2.

3.

Look at your answers. Is there a common thread? Maybe you see that you really want to reduce stress. Perhaps you need more rest. It could be that you seek more connections or improved relationships. The common thread in your answers will point to your *Why*. Write this down and post it somewhere you can see it every day—like your refrigerator, bathroom mirror, or by your desk. Make sure you see it every day so you can embody this desire and build momentum.

This *Why* will act as your anchor and will help you carve a path to your desired outcome. Write it here:

My Why Statement:

Download and print your Self-Healing Invitation here:

Declaring your *Why* is taking the very first step towards this beautiful version of you that you want to create. Being a healthy person and the best version of yourself isn't just physical. It's being aware of the mind-body connection so that we can work on all aspects of ourselves, including the emotional and spiritual sides. We'll take a look at this holistic approach to health next.

Chapter 2: A Holistic Approach to Healing

Holistic healing is an approach that considers the interconnectedness of the physical, emotional, and spiritual aspects of a person's life. It emphasizes the importance of balance and harmony to achieve optimal health and well-being. If one area is out of balance, it can directly or indirectly affect the order and balance of the others. This is when health issues can arise.

Holistic healing has been around for centuries, but as people consider their health needs more closely, more and more are changing their perspectives on what optimal health means to them and are willing to try alternative health solutions.

Six years into my recovery from alcohol use, I became fascinated by holistic wellness. I was first introduced to pure essential oils in 2017 and discovered a more natural way to treat my stress-related issues. Using plant medicine to heal in conjunction with other holistic modalities like meditation, reiki, and healing sound baths completely won me over. I became obsessed. It was then that I knew my calling was to serve others in this way and show them an alternative way to treat their stress and anxiety.

When I started making the oils a regular part of my health regime, I immediately noticed how well they worked. I was sleeping better, my mood stabilized, and my tendency to react to other people softened. Because of this impact on my mental well-being, I could focus better, interact with others with kindness and compassion, and perform better at my job.

I partnered with the wellness company so that I could educate and share the essential oils and products with others. Soon, I found myself surrounded by holistic health enthusiasts who not only led with their hearts but approached health differently. From there, I expanded into health coaching and teaching mindfulness meditation while incorporating essential oils into every area of my practice.

Read more about how essential oils can calm anxious feelings here:

Natural healing solutions were getting a lot more attention during the 2020 pandemic. The pandemic contributed to a broader conversation about holistic well-being and encouraged individuals to consider holistic approaches to their health and wellness, which have been around for years. The spotlight on natural health included conversations around:

1. **Holistic approaches**: The pandemic heightened people's awareness of the need for balance among physical, mental, and emotional well-being.
2. **Immune health:** The pandemic brought to light a huge focus on immunity, leading to more conversations around natural ways to boost the immune system through nutrition, supplements, and lifestyle changes.
3. **Emotional and mental well-being**: The pandemic's impact on mental health led to a surge of interest in different ways to manage stress and anxiety, including meditation, mindfulness, and breathwork as powerful tools for emotional well-being.
4. **Holistic nutrition**: People are perhaps more conscious of their diets, opting for foods that are whole foods, organic, and locally

sourced. There has been a growing interest in the connection between nutrition and overall health.

5. **Home-based fitness**: With lockdowns and restrictions in place, people exercised out of boredom using home-based fitness routines such as yoga, Pilates, and bodyweight exercises. These practices often incorporate holistic principles that promote physical and mental well-being.

6. **Herbal medicine and natural remedies**: There has been a resurgence of interest in herbal medicine and natural remedies to support chronic illness, disease, and pain, such as herbal supplements, teas, and other holistic approaches like acupuncture and reiki.

7. **Community and support networks**: The pandemic highlighted the importance of community and social support for well-being. Holistic health practitioners and groups offered virtual support and resources for individuals seeking a sense of community and connection.

The pandemic gave wellness advocates like me an opportunity to educate more and more people looking for ways to prevent rather than treat viruses and diseases and to explore alternative ways to heal and enhance their overall health and wellness.

Understanding your current health is the first step in creating a foundation for a personalized plan tailored to your unique needs and long-term vision. Some health coaches will use a comprehensive questionnaire when privately working with clients. I like to start with a more visual approach called the holistic health wheel. This exercise was designed for individuals who want a personalized wellness program but are unsure of where and how to start. By calling out specific areas of health that are out of balance, we can simplify the journey ahead by focusing on two to three areas first, more easily establish intentions for our health, and create some specific health habits and lifestyle modifications to help get back to balance.

I like this simplified approach of the holistic health wheel because it can help you to go from feeling overwhelmed in the beginning to more in control of your health as we move forward. Health is comprehensive, but we want to break it down into manageable bite-size pieces to fulfill your intentions.

Why do I say *intentions* and not *goals*? When we set intentions for ourselves, there is an immediate connection. An intention is something we can set daily that can help move us towards a goal, such as emotional balance, weight loss, or financial freedom. This process of recovering, healing, and thriving is a journey, not a quest to get to the destination and then stop. Daily intentions keep us moving in the direction of where we want to go and in how we want to feel.

When I got sober, no one suggested I stop drinking, fix my relationships, change my eating habits, stop smoking, and start exercising all at once. It was one day at a time, one area of health at a time, until I achieved balance in my health physically, emotionally, and spiritually.

Self-Healing Invitation: Holistic Health Wheel

This is a great exercise I use with clients at the beginning of their programs to identify where they are out of balance in their lives and to establish a baseline. It's beneficial to practice this periodically so we can measure our progress or pinpoint where we need to focus our time and attention since, as we move through life, our experiences change. As we shift in our experiences, so do our health priorities. I practice this exercise quarterly so I can gauge where I'm at and how I am evolving and make any adjustments to my wellness protocols as needed. This also ensures that I am aligned with my long-term vision for health and wellness.

Before we dive into this exercise, let's stop and think about our long-term vision. Our vision isn't the same thing as our goals or intentions. It's the state of being we see ourselves in the long term. Who do you want to be? How do you want to feel? What do you want to be doing five or even ten years from now? Close your eyes and picture your future self. What do you see?

Take a few moments to describe your vision in the space here:

Now, let's complete the holistic health wheel. Follow the instructions and keep in mind where your current self is in all eight areas of the circle.

Where are you out of balance?

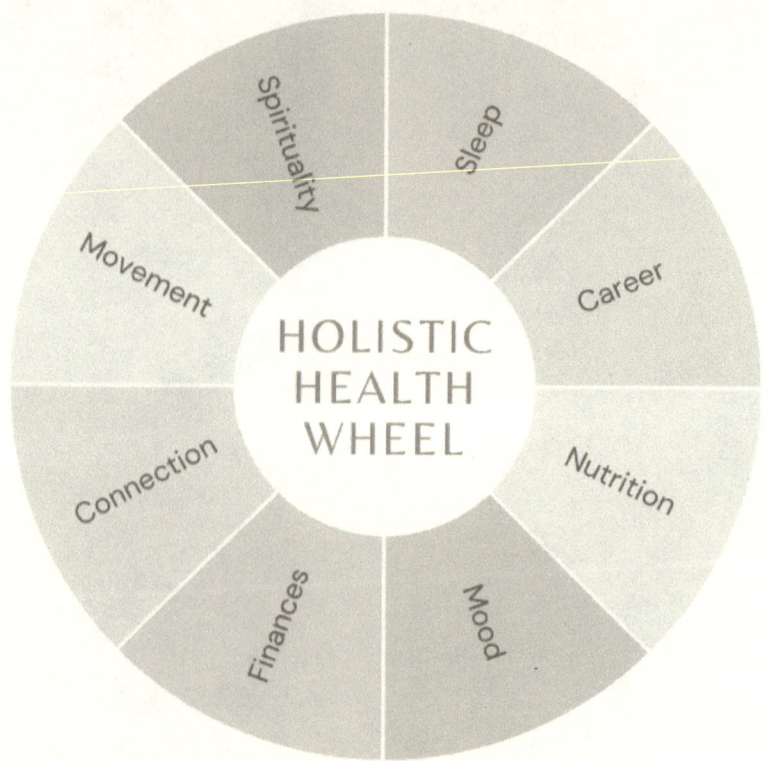

Instructions:

1. Rate each area of health in the health wheel on a scale from 1-10, with one being the least satisfied and 10 being the most satisfied. Don't overthink it. What number immediately comes to mind? You'll receive the answers from your intuitive mind faster than your thinking mind, so write down the first number that pops into your head. Simply place your number within each piece of the pie.

2. Connect your numbers around the pie chart like you're connecting the dots. Notice the shape. Is it perfectly round, or is there a lot of zig-zagging? The more zig-zags, the more imbalance.

3. Now, let's focus on the actual rating. Fill in the chart below with both your current ratings and the ratings of where you would like to be. Your rating can be the same for both columns. There are no right or wrong answers.

Areas of the Health Wheel	Where I Am Now	Where I Want to Be
Spirituality		
Sleep		
Career		
Nutrition		
Mood		
Finances		
Connection		
Movement		

Where are the three largest gaps between where you are and where you want to be?

Where are there the smallest gaps?

Identifying your gaps will help you get clear on what specific actions will support your long-term vision for health and wellness. For example, the last time I did this exercise, I had a pretty big gap in the area of connection. I had been at home for a good year writing and coaching, and I wasn't getting out and nurturing relationships. I was a hermit. I was isolating myself and working. After seeing the gap, I set an intention to make conversations and relationships outside of the house more of a priority. I needed it, and my business needed it. This exercise gave me this awareness.

With this information, you can go deeper and assess the lifestyle choices that might be causing the gap. Once we uncover those, we have a place to start in making some lifestyle modifications and better choices that will shift both your physical and emotional state. If we use this exercise periodically, we are being proactive about our health, putting us back in control and able to manage the imbalances better when they are happening. Ideally, we want to strive for complete harmony on the health wheel.

Three intentions for my health and wellness are:

1.

2.

3.

The health wheel can be beneficial in giving you the awareness you need as you continue reading through the parts of this book. You will gain perspective on where your gaps are and apply what you learn to close those gaps and create more life balance.

Download and print your Self-Healing Invitation here:

Now, let's take your awareness and move into part two—*Mindset and Mindfulness.*

MINDSET AND MINDFULNESS

Chapter 3: Cultivating Mindfulness

"Mindfulness is a pause—the space between stimulus and response: that's where choice lies." — Tara Brach

Towards the end of my drinking, I felt like I was stuck at the bottom of a well, staring up at the tiny hole way at the top where I could see blue sky and clouds moving effortlessly—and all I could think was, *how will I ever get out?* My drinking had reached the stage where it was a physical compulsion. I could not function without it, and if I tried, I would get physically sick. It was holding me prisoner.

When I sobered up and went to live at the homeless shelter where I had my surrender, I realized I was no longer sitting in that well. This was a way out, and I didn't have to feel trapped anymore. I had that moment of pause while sitting in the lobby, waiting to get checked in, and noticed how I felt. As scared as I was, there were butterflies in my belly, the kind I would get when I knew something really good was about to happen, like waking up on Christmas morning with the anticipation of finding that gift you asked Santa for. It was a surge of excitement at the thought of being free from this incomprehensible demoralization. For the first time in years, I felt hopeful, not hopeless, and everything started to look different.

At that moment, I made a choice. I was done with alcohol. Everything was forward-moving after that. Growth, expansion, and transformation followed.

While I may not have realized it at the time, what I experienced was a moment of extraordinary spiritual mindfulness. Mindfulness is simply how we pay attention to the present moment and how we cultivate awareness through a mind-body connection. This deep connection between the mind and body can empower us to make choices that are good for us and pave the way for transformation. The sensations I felt running through my body that day were a signal to my brain that something good was happening. And because I stopped to take notice and examine, I became aware that I was excited at the prospect of change, so the surrender came instantly.

Let's dive a little deeper into what mindfulness is, why it's important, and how it serves as the foundation for growth and expansion.

Thoughts → Feelings → Actions → Habits

Our thoughts create feelings, which influence our actions, which become our habits and our way of being. If we want to change our way of being and how we are showing up in the world, we first need to revisit our thoughts. When we notice our thoughts, we practice mindfulness.

Without my sobriety, I wouldn't have had a transformative journey. It was the very first step I took towards reclaiming my health and taking back control of my life. While I was stuck in my disease, I had a mindset of lack, and I couldn't imagine my life without alcohol. It was my security blanket, and I thought I needed it to get through everything, like a date, a job interview, or even going to the grocery store. I grabbed for it like a reflex, without pausing to question. It wasn't just a bad habit. It was my solution for everything, and I didn't have an identity without it.

That day I arrived at the homeless shelter was the first day I was mindful of my situation. I had a moment to pause, feel, and choose how to respond. When I was drinking, there was no pause. There wasn't even an awareness of time. I didn't stop before raising the bottle to my mouth to consider the consequences of my actions—jail, job loss, family conflict, bankruptcy. There was complete ignorance of the damage I was doing to myself or how it was impacting others; not once did I stop to think about how I was breaking their hearts each time they found me drunk.

Mindfulness and the hope, humility, and gratitude I felt that day saved my life. The practice can help us break through blocks, cultivate awareness, become more self-confident, make better life decisions, and heal from trauma. Mindfulness was my key to getting unstuck and taking back control of my life so I could freely thrive in health and happiness.

As one of the most effective tools available, mindfulness helps shift negative thinking and shapes the outcomes we seek. Always within our reach, this practice can guide us toward transformation, reducing anxiety, or boosting productivity in any area of life.

When I first started learning mindfulness, most notably at the shelter, I experienced a profound change within myself rather quickly. Mindfulness taught me that there was always something to be grateful for, even at the worst of times. It was a way for me to focus on something other than my anxiety and step into a safe space in my mind.

I remember experiencing this on my early morning bike rides to my recovery meetings. I didn't have a driver's license at the time, so I either rode my bike or took it with me on the bus if it was raining. Noticing and appreciating the small things along my ride, like a flower, the sunrise, or a morning breeze, and learning what it felt like to be truly humble and grateful for these experiences reframed my thinking from feeling trapped to feeling free.

My rides became less about getting somewhere and more about connecting with myself and God. Beautiful views surrounded me—the sunrise casting an ombre of pinks, oranges, and reds, the Gulf of Mexico with its powdery sandy beaches, perfectly landscaped golf courses, palm trees, and lush tropical gardens. Wildlife was everywhere—birds, owls, lizards, turtles, ducks, otters, egrets, and even flamingos. When it was quiet, I could hear a chorus of them singing all around me if I listened closely. I lived in paradise, and I never really stopped to appreciate it.

Since I didn't have a driver's license, riding my bike to get where I needed to go began to feel transformative. Naples, Florida, where I lived, wasn't a bike-friendly city at that time. One local bus had limited stops, so it was not easy to get around if you didn't have a car. Still, over time, I was able to flip the script on something I once complained about and stopped feeling so sorry for myself.

Instead of thinking, *"I have to ride my bike. What if someone I know sees me riding my bike? It's going to take me forever to get places on my bike,"* my attitude shifted to, *"I get to ride my bike. I'm grateful I have my bike. I get great exercise riding my bike."* What many would consider an inconvenience, I came to see as something liberating. For once, I was able to take care of my own needs and show up where I needed to be without relying on someone else. I finally felt independent, like an adult—something I hadn't felt in years.

Thanks to my bike for getting me places, I landed a job at a clothing store in an upscale outdoor shopping center near the beach. It was my first "get well" job—a term we use in recovery to describe starting over with work that doesn't cause undue pressure or emotional demand, allowing recovery to remain the main focus.

This job taught me a lot about myself, starting with relearning responsibility. I hadn't held a job for more than a few months at a time in over three years. Although I was offered rides to and from work by others who lived at the shelter and had cars, I decided not to take the easy way out and rode my bike. I always packed clean clothes in my backpack so I could change in a public bathroom when I got to my destination. It was the middle of summer, and I was usually pretty sweaty after the 45-minute ride.

When it rained, I took the bus. I could catch the local bus at the Government Center, right down the road from the shelter. At first, I was leery of the bus because, after all, this was Naples, not New York City. People in Naples didn't typically have to worry about bus schedules. After a while though, I grew to enjoy my time on the bus. It gave me moments to sit quietly with myself, which brought a sense of calm and mindfulness into my day. These rides became an opportunity to reflect and stay present, helping me reconnect with myself and my purpose. It reminded me of the days when I commuted into New York City. The energy of getting to work on time or catching the train at the end of the day made me feel like someone important with a purpose and somewhere to be.

Another thing I learned about myself was that I enjoyed and was good at engaging with people. I'd been disconnected for so long that I convinced myself that I was scared of people and could never work a client-facing job. The more I showed up and put myself out there, being of service as my most authentic self, I squashed this limiting belief, connecting with people with ease. In moments where I just wanted to keep my head down, I would remind myself that when I smiled and said hello, something inside of me lit up. It energized me and brought me to life. And the more I did it, the more I came out of my shell. I practiced it over and over until I got so good at creating relationships that I got promoted to a management position.

I felt supported by my work team. No one questioned me about riding my bike to work or using a backpack instead of a purse. During my interview, I told my manager about my DUI because I had noted on my application that I'd been arrested. She asked me about it and hired me anyway. She told me she respected my honesty, so she gave me a chance. I didn't know at the time, but this chance opportunity was the first step into a 10-year career as a store manager. No one there ever treated me differently; they always made me feel like a valued member of the team. It had been a long time since I felt that way. Perhaps this was my God putting me right where I needed to be right when I needed it.

When I stopped drinking, my entire world opened up. These first experiences of riding my bike and working my first job were opportunities to soak in the moment and notice what was happening both inside and outside myself. For such a long time, it had just been me, my bottle, and where I was getting my next drink. I never noticed the chirping of birds or the way the sky looked different every morning at sunrise. I didn't pay attention to how my body felt when I was so anxious I wanted to die. I numbed myself to my emotions, so there was never any self-awareness, not until I got sober.

After about four months of living at the shelter, I'd saved enough money to put a deposit on an apartment. Once again, I enjoyed the luxury of having my own private bedroom and bathroom. Although I had grown accustomed to sleeping in a dorm with 20 other women, like at summer camp, I realized just how much I appreciated my own space. My bike remained my primary mode of transportation, but now, the ride to work was shorter. There was a bus stop across the street, but I still preferred riding my bike, only using the bus if it was raining.

In the winter months, it could get cold at night. I'd bundle up and ride home from work and smile the whole way, often riding faster than the cars. The cool air on my face felt invigorating, always giving me a rush of adrenaline. I can't recall a single time riding my bike when I felt self-pity. "People commute this way all over the world," I reminded myself. "This isn't any different."

Bringing mindfulness to a moment instead of frustration opened me up to receive more feelings of freedom. This liberation was of paramount importance because I had been living in my own prison for such a long time. I was finding true happiness within, simply from riding my bike. How freeing it was to know that no matter what was happening in the world around me, I had the power to remain happy and in peace.

Mindfulness is how we show up to every moment of our lives. It's how we pay attention to the moment we are in. It's learning how to become conscious of our awareness. When mindful, we have an opportunity to bring awareness to our experiences and make each moment meaningful.

When I made the decision not to drink, I created space for transformation. The mindfulness and self-awareness of that moment allowed me to set a foundation for my sobriety that I could build upon. I took one step at a time, and new doors kept opening for me to further explore and expand on this new holistic path. Mindfulness became a daily practice for me, and as a result, I cultivated gratitude and an eagerness to make more lifestyle modifications, one at a time, that would help me achieve the health, wealth, and happiness I finally knew I deserved.

Mindfulness = Awareness = Transformation

One way I love to practice mindfulness that really helped me at the beginning of my sobriety was through mindfulness meditation. Mindfulness meditation is an effective way to become more mindful and is typically practiced for one of three reasons:

1) Intervention for anxiety or pain
2) Transformation
3) A tool to improve performance in one or more areas of life

In a study published on August 21, 2024, in the *British Journal of Health Psychology* (Vol. 29, Issue 4, pp. 1091-1048), researchers found that just ten minutes of daily mindfulness practice can improve well-being, ease depression and anxiety, and motivate more people to improve their lifestyle. Most of the participants in the study had no prior experience with mindfulness and were either given a month-long mindfulness routine or a control condition. Mindfulness exercises were delivered via a free mobile application. Some of the key findings from those using the mindfulness app were:

1. Reduced depression by 19.2% more than the control group.
2. Improved well-being by 6.9%.
3. Decreased anxiety by 12.6%.

4. Attitudes to health were more positive by 7.1% over the control group.
5. Behavioral intentions to look after health increased by 6.5% beyond the control group.

Brief moments of mindfulness can be a powerful step towards reclaiming your health and creating more joy in your life, and it's available to us wherever and whenever we need it. When we first start, we may need to consciously set aside time to practice things like deep breathing, meditation, a nutritious meal, or a walk in nature until it becomes our way of being.

The key to making mindfulness work for us is consistent practice so we can create habits that stick. As we learn to weave it into our daily lives, we cultivate more awareness, from which transformation begins to unfold. It is with this awareness that we can consciously contemplate what is best for us.

Mindfulness and Our Health

Why is mindfulness so good for our health?

First, mindfulness helps us manage our stress. Stress triggers the release of cortisol, impacting hormonal balance. Elevated cortisol can suppress the immune system, affecting its ability to defend against illness. Chronic stress may also disrupt cellular function and contribute to inflammation, further emphasizing the importance of stress management for overall health.

Mindfulness encourages positive bodily change when it comes to our hormones, immunity, cellular aging, and inflammation. A simple daily practice for ten minutes a day, when done consistently, can significantly reduce health risks over time.

It's important to note that a mindfulness practice is not a cure for any disease or chronic illness but can teach us how to adapt and be more resilient. Mindfulness has been shown to improve mental health and physical symptoms associated with chronic illness, anxiety, depression, and pain. By recognizing that we have a choice in matters of our health, we can start to steer our transformation in the direction we want it to go, one step at a time.

So, how can we bring more mindfulness into our day?

An easy way to incorporate mindfulness more regularly is by habit stacking. You can practice mindfulness at any point during the day while in other routines or doing other tasks, such as when you're taking a shower, exercising, folding laundry, or driving to work. Being mindful in moments such as these can enhance your experience and bring you a sense of presence and peace. So many of us are used to running on autopilot, and we don't think we can use our daily routines to our advantage in this way. We're thinking about our to-do lists, project deadlines, and how we're going to make dinner, do the laundry, and get the kids to and from sports practice. These small moments get lost, and we miss precious opportunities that can significantly contribute to our personal growth.

According to some experts, people operate on autopilot for almost half their lives. This means that for half our lives, we are not in full control. That's a scary thought. Being on autopilot steals precious downtime from us that we could use to refresh and rejuvenate our minds and bodies.

Picture this: It's a beautiful day outside. You're walking your dog like you routinely do, but your mind is on tomorrow's meeting. You start thinking about what could go wrong or what people will think of your presentation, which leads you to think about what you are going to wear and whether it's cleaned and pressed, which leads you to remember the three loads of laundry you haven't started yet and what the heck you're going to make for dinner. As you connect one thought to another, you find yourself worrying about whether you'll be able to sleep that night or what if you forget to set your alarm. So, you make a mental note to set your alarm as soon as you get back to the house. But what are you making for dinner again? As your dog pulls at the leash and you come back to the moment, you don't even know if your dog did her business or not because you've been down your rabbit hole the whole time.

Walking the dog could have been a great way to recharge. The sun was shining, the breeze was gentle, the birds were singing, and the dog was great company. But the moment was missed. There was no break from the mental chaos.

Setting an intention to be present with the simplest of tasks allows you to fully appreciate the sensations, scents, and sounds, offering a refreshing break for recharging your mind and body. Practicing the mindfulness techniques that we will explore throughout this book enables you to change the hardwiring of your brain, making it easier and more natural for you to live in the moment, make better choices, create new health habits, and free yourself from the self-sabotaging behaviors that have been making you feel stuck.

Bringing mindfulness to our daily lives can be a transformative experience. The practice can lead to shifts in our mindset that can alter our perspectives, beliefs, or attitudes, leading to a new way of thinking and, even more, a new way of being.

As you begin to make some small lifestyle modifications with mindfulness, not only will the way you view yourself and the world change, but so will the way you show up for yourself and others. Let's try a few mindfulness exercises next.

Self-Healing Invitation: Mindfulness Journaling

Take an inventory of how much time you spend on moments outside of the present. Grab a notebook, and as you move throughout your day, try making a note of every time you catch your mind wandering. As you make your list, capture where your mind actually goes.

What are you thinking about?

What are you feeling?

Did the thought align with what you were doing at the moment?

Are you experiencing high anxiety, frustration, or anger?

How is your breathing? Is it steady or fast and short?

Where can you feel the sensations in your body when anxiety comes up?

Just notice without judgment and make a note of those observations for one whole day. As you go throughout your week, practice catching yourself in these moments and pull yourself back in. Focus on your breathing. Take a few deep breaths in through the nose and even longer breaths out through the mouth. Set an intention, saying it to yourself with each breath in, and then as you breathe out, let go of any thoughts that don't serve you. Notice any difference in how you feel.

Download and print your Self-Healing Invitation here:

Self-Healing Invitation: Mindfulness Teeth Brushing

Now, let's try a short practice that shows us how mindfulness can turn an everyday habit into a meaningful one. Let's engage in mindfully brushing our teeth.

Brushing our teeth is a habit we've adopted since the minute we could hold a toothbrush. It's typically done mechanically, without giving it too much thought. But mindlessly brushing our teeth can actually do more harm than good. Sure, brushing our teeth is necessary to fight cavities and tooth decay, but when we don't pay attention, we could damage our gums, experience plaque buildup, and end up with gum disease. How many of you have brushed, not realizing how hard you are on your gums? Then you go to the dentist and find out that the damage is done. How we pay attention to brushing our teeth is more important than the brushing part because it creates awareness of our oral health.

For the next week, try to be present as you brush your teeth. Instead of dreading this exercise, anticipate it as a time for some self-care. Turn it into a pleasant experience by tuning in to all the senses while you brush. The rule of thumb is to brush for a full two minutes, so set a timer, put on some music, and brush mindfully. Be attentive and aware of the experience without judgment.

Reflect on these questions:

1. How does the pressure feel on your gums?

2. How does the toothpaste taste?

3. What are the different sensations in your mouth? Maybe it's tingling or burning.

4. What is the texture of the toothpaste?

5. Are the bristles on your toothbrush soft or hard?

6. Is the water warm or cold?

7. How do your teeth look when you are done?

8. How do you feel when you're done?

9. How do your teeth feel when you run your tongue over them?

Afterward, journal about your experience and answer these questions below:

1. Did this practice make you aware of anything new?

2. Were there opportunities for adjustments?

3. Did you notice a shift in attitude with regard to brushing your teeth?

4. Were you able to stay mindful throughout the practice?

5. Did how you perceive brushing your teeth shift in any way?

Download and print your Self-Healing Invitation here:

Maybe nothing changed for you, and that's OK. This was just a practice for you to see how bringing mindfulness to a daily habit could potentially shift your mindset and turn that habit into an act of self-care. It's intentionally focusing on a behavior without judgment so that you can be your best self. Although we're all used to brushing our teeth morning and night (hopefully without fail), we aren't used to being present with the behavior and noticing all of the positive or negative sensations that can arise. We miss the moment we are in, which can cause us to overlook something that may need our care and attention. Bringing mindfulness to our daily brush is an act of self-love.

You can bring this mindfulness practice to other activities you enjoy to create healthier lifestyle modifications. Repeating the behaviors in ten-minute daily increments will help the brain strengthen the connections associated with the new behavior, turning it into a new, healthy habit that you'll do without a second thought.

What daily habit or habits will you apply mindfulness to? If you're stuck, here are a few ideas of how you can bring mindfulness to your day and shut down autopilot mode:

1. Mindful movement like walking, stretching, or a yoga sequence.
2. Set an alarm on your phone or use an Alexa device to remind you to stop and do a ten-minute mindfulness practice.
3. Bring mindfulness to a task like doing the laundry, emptying the dishwasher, or vacuuming. Use the steps from the teeth brushing exercise above, or just allow your mind to rest and see what arises.

4. Try a different route to work or to pick your kids up from school. This trains your mind to break patterns and habits, creating space to create new ones.

5. Put that one thing you've been putting off onto your calendar to break the pattern of procrastination caused by being on autopilot.

6. Have designated device-free time. Put your phone in another room or leave it at home if you're running a quick errand to give yourself time to be present without constant distractions.

7. Try to be spontaneous. Grab a friend for coffee or dinner, sign up for a yoga class, or take an afternoon to visit your local zoo or botanical garden.

Self-Healing Invitation: Ten Minutes of Mindfulness

These ten-minute mindfulness practices can be easily incorporated into your daily routine, even during busy days, to help you shift your mindset towards a more positive and centered state of being. Find one or two that work for you and practice it consistently for two weeks. I recommend journaling on your reflections after each practice.

- **Mindful breathing**: Take three minutes to focus on your breath. Inhale deeply for four seconds, hold for four seconds, exhale slowly for four seconds, and hold for four seconds. Pay attention to the sensation of each breath to calm your mind. Notice how the breath feels as it flows in and out. Resume a natural breath while staying mindful and just sit with it for the remaining seven minutes.

- **Body scan**: Spend ten minutes scanning your body from head to toe. Find a comfortable seat or lay down, and start from your head and move down towards your toes. Notice any areas of tension or discomfort without judgment and consciously relax them. As you move down your body, say the body part out loud as you place your focus on it. Ex: "*arm; belly; thigh.*"

- **Gratitude list**: Spend ten minutes writing a gratitude list. Your list might look the same every day or not. This can help you cultivate a positive and thankful mindset. Gratitude is the highest vibration you can be in. You can't feel like a victim and be grateful at the same time.

- **Meditation**: Dedicate ten minutes to a short meditation, focusing on a positive intention, affirmation, or simply clearing your mind. You can find great meditations on apps such as Calm, Chopra, Insight Timer, or DailyOm. I've also created a playlist of meditations for you on my resource page.

- **Spend time in nature**: Step outside and spend ten minutes observing nature, like watching the clouds, listening to birds, or feeling the breeze. Root your feet into the ground to help you feel supported. Hug a tree to get grounded.

- **Mindful eating**: Eat a small snack or meal slowly and mindfully, savoring each bite and appreciating the flavors, smells, and textures. This practice can be out of our comfort zone because it may feel unnatural to place so much focus on each bite and swallow. But it forces us to slow down, practice patience, and cultivate awareness.

- **Quick stretching**: Engage in a brief stretching or yoga routine, paying attention to the sensations in your muscles as you move, promoting physical and mental relaxation. Notice the release you feel from the stretch, relief from pain, or any tightness in areas of your body.

- **Mini-visualization**: Spend ten minutes visualizing a positive outcome or a place of calm and serenity, allowing your mind to focus on positive imagery. Sit quietly with your eyes closed and just let yourself indulge in a daydream. This is a great manifesting practice, so focus on something you truly desire.

- **Affirmation break**: Take a few moments to repeat a positive affirmation or mantra that resonates with you, reinforcing a positive mindset. Positive affirmations can reframe negative thinking and alter your self-beliefs. They help you to change the way you see yourself. They give you doses of self-love. They can change your script about your life.

- **Free writing:** Ten minutes of journaling in a free writing fashion can help you release and discover truths about yourself. Write down whatever comes up. Journaling can help us heal by allowing us to reveal to ourselves the root cause of an issue through our writing. Our subconscious minds step forward here and allow deep-rooted feelings and beliefs to rise to the surface for us to see and examine.

Download and print your Self-Healing Invitation here:

Chapter 4: Bully Voices

Growing up, I was my own worst enemy. My thoughts constantly swirled around fears of failure and rejection: *What if I fail? What if I lose? What if they don't like me?* These questions were a relentless loop in my mind, making me feel panicked and hyperventilating under the pressure I put on myself. My inner voice was a bully, endlessly repeating that I wasn't smart enough, thin enough, pretty enough, or good enough. In my quest to prove it wrong, I wore myself out trying to be the best at everything. Anything less than perfection felt like a failure.

One moment that stands out was during my senior year of high school. I was under immense pressure to maintain an undefeated record in my singles position on the tennis team. But then I faced an undefeated opponent from another school who ended up destroying me. Once my score was down, I couldn't recover. The match was lost in my mind long before it was lost on the court. Anxiety choked my ability to breathe, and my self-doubt ensured I couldn't crawl my way back. Had I believed in myself, the outcome might have been different.

When it came to my studies, I was in every advanced class. I'd double my own workload just to keep up. Many nights, I'd find myself in the basement, burning the midnight oil, memorizing textbook passages, and rewriting my notes. When I think back on it, the amount I worked was pure madness. I envied classmates who breezed through exams with top marks while I overthought every question. Our science teacher's habit of celebrating the high achievers in front of the whole class and subtly shaming those who didn't make the grade only fueled my obsession. Looking back, I realize I might have been happier if I hadn't insisted on staying in those advanced classes, but I was determined to prove my worth.

The biggest blow came when I didn't get into my dream college—my dad's alma mater. Since childhood, we'd visit for football games, and I dreamed of being a student and rallying in the stands with pride and spirit. I was obsessed about getting in, worried that my SAT scores wouldn't make the cut. When the acceptance letters came, mine wasn't among them. Instead, the girl who ranked second in our high school class got in, and I was devastated. It felt like she had taken my spot. Humiliated, I could hardly speak to her for the rest of the year, not out of anger but because I felt so ashamed. Everyone knew I wanted to go there, and I had failed to get in.

Your bully voice is responsible for your limiting beliefs. It creates stories that diminish your self-confidence. It's the voice that tells you, "You can't, you suck, and you'll never be something.

The voice inside me screamed, *"You're not good enough,"* after getting that rejection letter, and it continued to beat me down for years. I operated on the belief that I always needed to *do more, produce more, and be more* to be loved and accepted. This story I told myself slowly chipped away at my self-confidence and sense of self-worth and deprived me of relishing in the moments when I was winning at life. I was always so focused on doing things perfectly and excessively that I couldn't even enjoy the moment I was in most of the time.

This inner bully was the source of my limiting beliefs. The bully thrives on negativity, feeding us lies that keep us stuck in self-doubt and fear, blocking us from seeing opportunities and moving forward. The bully voice is sneaky, embedding itself in our thoughts from childhood and growing louder and more convincing as we age. It can become so powerful that we start to believe the lies it tells us, and we spend years of our lives settling for mediocrity because we don't think we deserve or can do any better.

The first time I can recall this bully voice was when I was around 13 years old. It was a Saturday, and I was running errands with my dad in his new cherry red convertible. I loved those rides, especially in the early days of fall when the air was crisp but the sun was still warm. My dad was my hero—a successful Wall Street man who had retired early, and I felt proud to be by his side.

That day, as I waited in the car while my dad picked up dry cleaning, a truck with two young guys pulled up next to me. They turned to look at me, or so I thought. Summoning the courage, I smiled, not wanting to seem snobby. But then I heard one of them say, "We're not looking at *you*. We're looking at the car!" They laughed, and I froze.

At that moment, the bully voice took over. *"They're right,"* it sneered. *"Who are you to think they'd be looking at you? You're just a thirteen-year-old geek with no boobs, a boy's haircut, and big feet. You're not even cute!"* My face flushed with shame. If I could've driven, I would have sped away, leaving my dad to find his way home. I was mortified, feeling small, ugly, and unimportant.

That single comment haunted me for years. It became a loop in my mind, replaying whenever I felt vulnerable. As I grew older, it became harder to make eye contact with men. I started drinking just to feel comfortable around them, to silence the voice that told me I wasn't good enough. I rushed into relationships, desperate for validation, terrified that no one would want me. That comment and the bully voice that followed planted a seed of insecurity that shaped how I saw myself for years.

They weren't the only ones who teased me. I got mocked at school because I was taller than my brothers and had a size 10 shoe. My mom insisted on taking me to the barber shop with my brothers to get a pixie haircut because she liked my hair short, and it was easier to get our cuts all at once. I felt like a boy, not a girl. Some of the boys called me a "goon" because of my height and picked on me for having big feet. One boy, Josh, teased me so much that one day, I took my "big" foot and stomped on his. I don't remember him teasing me much after that. The word "goon" stuck with me for a long time, reinforcing the idea that I was big, awkward, and unattractive.

The funny thing is, I wasn't actually big. I was just tall with big feet. But in my mind, I felt enormous in my body and minuscule in my confidence. The bully voice was relentless, whispering the words from those boys in my ear, *"Nice feet. What, are they a size 13?"*

By the time I was 17, I thought the answer to my problems was a crash diet. I believed that being skinny would make me feel comfortable in my skin. If I were skinny and pretty, I'd never have to worry about being mocked again.

I remember the night I made this decision. It was during the holidays, and my family was hosting a dinner party. There was always so much food, and it was good food, too, because my Italian mother really knew how to cook. I couldn't control myself with all the desserts. I loved my sweets; there were cookies, cannoli, chocolates, and cheesecake. I couldn't resist the homemade Christmas cookies; we only made them once a year.

After I finished stuffing my face, like I enjoyed doing every holiday season, I was suddenly hit with feelings of extreme remorse. I excused myself from the table and went to my room. I was so full. I felt like throwing up. I remember looking in the mirror with this feeling of self-loathing, calling myself disgusting. I lifted my shirt and looked at my bulging stomach. *"This is so gross! How could you do this to yourself? How are you going to fix this?"* The very next day, I made a conscious decision to eat less. A lot less. It was my first step down a dangerous path of disordered eating.

I kept my new "scarcity diet" a secret for as long as I could. I skipped breakfast, reduced my lunch to a small salad, and barely touched dinner. Dinner was always a family affair at my house and the largest meal of the day, so I was petrified I wouldn't get away with eating practically nothing. My mom prepared heavy Italian and Hungarian dishes like pasta carbonara, sausage and peppers, chicken paprikash, and meatloaf. I became obsessed with calories, even telling my family I wanted to be a vegetarian to avoid her cooking. When the weight started dropping, I felt euphoric—light, attractive, confident, and in control.

I started exercising in my basement, running in place, running up and down the stairs, riding our stationary bike, and whatever else I could do to burn calories. But the food deprivation wore on me, and soon, I turned to binging and purging. It was a way to eat without guilt, to maintain control over my body. This pattern continued for years, well into my twenties, and I never considered the toll it was taking on my health. The bully voice had convinced me that this was the only way to feel better about myself.

My eating disorder progressed during college, and when I came home for Christmas break my senior year, my family staged an intervention. I was the thinnest I had ever been, and my parents' reaction when they saw me was anything but joyful. My brother, always my voice of reason, sat me down and told me how worried he was. His words cut through the fog of self-deception, and for the first time, I saw myself clearly.

After our conversation, I remember looking at a picture that was taken not long before. I was wearing a flannel shirt and black leggings, sitting next to our fireplace. Obviously, I'd looked at the picture plenty of times before, but when I looked at it this time, all I could see were those skinny stick legs. I didn't even recognize myself. If anyone else had tried to talk to me, I would have brushed them off, but my brother spoke from a place of love and compassion. He was non-judgmental. His words helped me realize I needed help.

My parents were so worried they threatened to pull me out of school and put me in a hospital. The thought terrified me, so I agreed to see a therapist and work on healthier eating habits. I managed to gain a few pounds and graduate with honors, which I will share more about in the chapter, Eat to Nourish, but my obsession with food lingered for years.

Eating disorders are an addiction, just like my alcoholism, and require daily work. Like my alcoholism, I am never 100% recovered. I am always *recovering*. It's a daily reprieve, and my addictive mind still tells me things like, "You don't have a disease."

For years, I ran with what my bully voice told me because I didn't have the tools that I have today to soften it and allow for a more compassionate voice to come in. I struggled emotionally, never able to accept myself for who I was. I convinced myself I had to go to the best schools, earn multiple degrees, make a lot of money, work for the best companies, or be the skinniest one in the room. I needed to feel like I was the best child, the best student, and the best worker on the team. When I underperformed, I'd beat myself up.

Today, my mindfulness practice helps me notice my bully voice without getting too involved with it. I hear it, acknowledge it, and sometimes give it a name. By giving it a name, I can put some distance between us and make room for a more loving and compassionate thought to come in. Tuning into the present moment by pausing and noticing without judgment gives me time to choose a better-feeling thought. The more I've practiced this, the quieter the bully voice has become.

Practices to Set Us Free from the Bully Voice

The first time I did any kind of deep inner work on myself was in Alcoholics Anonymous (AA). I had been in and out of the rooms of recovery for years while I was still drinking, but it wasn't until my surrender at the homeless shelter that I decided to willingly work a recovery program. My program gave me a solid foundation for my healing journey upon which I could build a life I never imagined possible.

I had to get really honest with myself, and it was really scary. This is where I truly began to discover who I was. I had to confront the damage

I had done to myself and others. It felt like I was expelling the demons from my soul, and it was after working through this that I was able to open up at meetings and share my experience, strength, and hope with others. Making myself vulnerable diminished the shame, and today, although I did some pretty horrible things while drunk, I no longer carry that guilt and shame inside of me. I continue to pay this gift of sobriety forward in ways that you will learn throughout this book.

The process was both challenging and uncomfortable. There were moments when staring down at the truth I had written about myself in my journal felt almost unbearable. However, it was through this uncomfortable honesty that I began to accept and forgive myself for my past wrongdoings. I started to recognize the patterns of thoughts and beliefs that kept me drinking, and I uncovered the deep-seated fears I had about living my life in a different way. The lies I had told myself, which led to abusing my body through starvation, purging, and drinking, were laid bare. Through this work, I was able to trace my negative behaviors back to thoughts that had kept me from realizing my potential. It felt like a cleansing of my soul, though I had to first confront and feel the shame before I could forgive myself and finally let it go.

Taking an inventory of my thoughts and actions is a practice that I return to time and time again. I've found that a simple journaling practice allows me to continue this work daily, helping me stay on track and remain open and honest with myself as I continue to heal.

Another daily practice that is powerful at freeing us from our bully voice is writing a gratitude list. Gratitude can quickly shift our attitudes, heal an aching heart, and help us see things from a different perspective. Gratitude can be practiced anywhere, anytime, and in so many different ways.

I first noticed how powerful gratitude could be while living at the homeless shelter. I remember telling people I was living there and seeing their faces contort, like the face you'd make when passing by a garbage truck or dumpster. While my circumstances may have seemed unfortunate to them, I was grateful I had a bed to sleep in and food to eat. There was coffee in the morning. That in itself was gold!

I had structure to my day and responsibilities. I had a purpose. So, I was grateful because this was a huge step up for me mentally. The housing itself was just a casing. It was what was happening to me on the inside that mattered the most.

I hadn't been grateful for anything for a very long time. Alcoholism is a selfish disease, and I didn't care who I hurt or how I hurt them. I was only concerned with myself. For years, my mom allowed me to live with her rent-free. She drove me anywhere I needed to be since I didn't have a driver's license. She bought my food. And I never appreciated any of it. All I cared about was drinking so I could numb my anger, depression, and sadness. I spent all my time feeling sorry for myself instead of being grateful someone was taking care of my needs.

Starting my day in gratitude keeps me focused on what is good in my life rather than what's not so great. I can embrace what I do have, not dwell on what I don't have. When we focus on and give thanks for the abundance we do have, more abundance comes to us readily and easily.

Celebrate the Small Wins

In my first few weeks of sobriety, all I felt was gratitude. I was grateful to feel physically better, to feel free from emotional pain, and to simply be alive. I had a few near-death experiences while drinking and driving, and it still amazes me that I never hurt someone else or myself. That is something I am most grateful for to this day. I learned to be grateful for where I was in my recovery each day, even if I had just taken one small step. When I was on my bike, I learned to be grateful for what seemed like the small stuff, like the sun, the birds, and the feel of the air on my face. I became mindful of my surroundings and appreciated the beauty of the sunrise, the palm trees, and the beaches. There was a sense of pride in taking responsibility for my life, paying my own rent, working out my transportation to and from work, and living on a budget with my food stamps. I was slowly taking my power back, the power that alcohol had over me that kept me pinned down, unable to do any of these simple things. That empowerment moved me away from feeling like a person ill-equipped to handle life and shifted me into a mindset of gratitude. It was one of my biggest life lessons and how I learned to look at the glass half full instead of half empty.

Today, I write a gratitude list before my feet hit the floor in the morning. I set my alarm a few minutes early so I can grab my notebook and pen on my nightstand and write the first three things that come to mind while my mind is free and clear. Sometimes, I write the same three things for days. Oftentimes, new things come to mind, perhaps surfacing from a dream.

One of the reasons why practicing gratitude works so well is because we can't be in a state of gratitude and negativity at the same time. A negative thought may pop up, and we acknowledge that it's there. But we can't feel the energy of a negative thought and a positive thought at the same time. The brain has a limited capacity for attention, so it's scientifically impossible to dwell in negativity while actively appreciating and acknowledging gratitude.

Starting my day with gratitude using this practice left little room for my bully voice to come in and try to ruin my day. When I practiced consistently, I created a new habit and changed my thinking. My brain was now operating differently. I was changing my own wiring. This didn't mean that negative thoughts didn't still pop into my head, but it was no longer my default way of thinking first thing in the morning.

Practicing gratitude puts your focus on the positive aspects of your life and enhances your self-awareness, which can shift your mindset, activate the areas associated with well-being, and release feelings of limitation.

Self-Healing Invitation: Gratitude

The next time you find yourself stuck in negative thinking, try one of the following gratitude practices that only take a few minutes. Stay mindful during these exercises and notice any changes in your body and mind. Maybe you don't notice anything at first, and that's OK. You are right where you need to be. Training our minds to think differently takes time and practice.

1. **Gratitude journaling**: Write down what you are grateful for that brings you joy—big or small. Notice any shifts in your thinking.
2. **Mindful breathing with gratitude**: Take a few minutes to practice deep, mindful breathing. While doing so, think about things that make you smile or have made you happy over the years. Notice how that makes you feel. Breathe into that feeling.
3. **Gratitude letter**: Write a letter to yourself or someone else expressing gratitude. If writing to someone else, think of someone who has impacted your life. Keep the letter in a journal. The act of writing it down can elicit a sense of appreciation.
4. **Gratitude walk**: Take a walk without your phone and notice your surroundings. Acknowledge the beauty of nature, the warmth of the sun, or the fresh air. Express gratitude for the sensory experiences around you.
5. **Gratitude visualization**: Close your eyes and visualize a situation or achievement for which you are grateful. Engage your senses to make the visualization vivid. This can evoke positive emotions and break the cycle of negative thinking.
6. **Express your gratitude out loud**: At any given time, say it out loud! Feel it as you say it. Expressing yourself verbally is declaring that you are more grateful than you are deprived. Allow this to empower you.

We can express our gratitude in so many ways. In fact, this past weekend, I climbed a tree. In Florida, where I live, we have huge banyan trees that are easy to climb and lounge in. I was feeling a bit off-center, so I climbed this beautiful tree and sat in stillness, just gazing out at my lake. I felt gratitude for having this tree to take me back to my childhood, where I spent afternoons climbing trees, playing in streams, and making mud pies. Being in the tree brought back a sense of playfulness and innocence when life was easy and fun. I showed myself that life can be this way as an adult, too.

Download and print your Self-Healing Invitation here:

Chapter 5: Create a New Story

I recently spoke with a man who shared an incredible story about his wife. At 35, she was diagnosed with a very aggressive form of breast cancer and was given just six months to live. Instead of succumbing to fear or self-pity, she embraced every moment, waking up each day with the thought: "*How are we going to make today great?*" Together, she and her husband traveled and explored life's opportunities, not with an urgency that time would run out, but with grace, ease, and curiosity. She received treatment, stayed positive, and went into remission. Today, over thirty years later, she is still alive and thriving, and the cancer has never returned.

I was blown away by this remarkable story of recovery. This man's wife was facing death and chose to focus on how she could live her best life today, in this moment. "She's always had this pattern of thinking," he explained. "She's never been one to immediately think the worst. She's always embraced everything about her life, whether good or bad."

The truth is, most of us aren't naturally inclined to think like this woman, especially when faced with a serious illness or, even worse, death. This doesn't make us flawed; it simply makes us human. Perhaps this woman was a miracle, defying the odds simply by directing her thoughts. But I find it no coincidence that she used the power of her mind, not necessarily to heal herself because she thought it would, but to thrive in each moment she had. And she's still doing it. While it might not come naturally, the ability to shape our thoughts and responses is within our reach, often more than we realize.

Changing our inner dialogue and, ultimately, the stories we tell ourselves is a gradual process that takes patience, consistent self-reflection, and mindfulness. We've had years of talking to ourselves in a certain way and holding tight to certain beliefs that may not necessarily be true. This "rewiring" of thought processes involves self-awareness, open-mindedness, and intentional effort to uncover our stories and start to think in a way that will better serve us.

In the next Self-Healing Invitation, we'll go through five steps to create your new story. I use this practice regularly when I want to reframe my thinking around something and let go of my bully voice:

Step 1: Identify the bully voice

Step 2: Identify the patterns and the story beneath it

Step 3: Cross-examine the story

Step 4: Let go of the old story

Step 5: Create Your New Story

We can begin by simply becoming aware of our bully voice. But before I explain how to do this, let me tell you why this step of awareness is so important.

Just to reiterate, our thoughts create feelings that influence our actions, which then become our habits. When we have negative thought patterns on repeat, our actions will reflect that. If we want to change our habits, we need to change our thoughts. When we change our thoughts, we can change our stories. When we change our stories, we shape our future.

Remember the young men mocking me when I was sitting in my dad's Mercedes? My thoughts (*I'm ugly*) made me feel bad about myself (*I'm not good enough*), which influenced my actions (*to eat less*), which became my behavior (*disordered eating*). The stories I told myself, that I was a big and unattractive girl who would probably never be loved, caused me to behave in a way that led me down a path of self-destruction with my eating disorder and then, years later, my drinking. I believed that if I was thin, I'd be prettier and I'd be more popular. I also believed that I was more likable when I drank, which made it easier to feel like I fit in.

Creating a new story for ourselves can have a powerful impact on how we shape our lives. To shift from a place where we constantly beat ourselves up with negative self-talk to a position of strength where we fuel ourselves with compassion, good intentions, and self-love can be truly transformative. Now, let's walk through the five steps, from identifying our bully voice to creating a new story.

Self-Healing Invitation: The 5 Steps to Create Your New Story

Step 1. Identify the bully voice

The first step in changing our story is to pay attention to our inner dialogue throughout the day. I recommend carrying a small notebook or starting a section in your phone's Notes app to quickly jot down any thoughts that come up. You might not even realize the stories you're telling yourself. Try this exercise: when you catch your bully voice talking to you, pause and take a moment to examine it with curiosity. Invite it in, but don't play. Use my example of how I assign it a name to give yourself some distance from it. You can say, "Hello, anger; hello, jealousy; hello, self-pity." This practice can help you build self-awareness, which is the foundation for inspired action and positive change.

Step 2. Identify the patterns and the story beneath them

What patterns do you notice with your bully voice?

When do you notice your bully voice speaking to you? What's happening? Where are you?

What tone does your bully voice take with you?

What words does it use?

What is it specifically addressing about you?

How do these words make you feel in your body? What sensations do you feel?

What emotions come up for you when you hear this voice?

What actions might you take as a result of this voice speaking to you?

Once you have answered these questions, it may be easier to recognize the story you've been telling yourself. For me, after practicing this many times, it finally became clear that the story I had been telling myself on repeat was, "You aren't good enough and won't be loved and accepted unless you do more, be more, and produce more." I was never enough.

What story have you been telling yourself? Share it here.

Step 3. Cross-examine the story

We can take this a step further and challenge the story our bully voice is feeding to us. When we cross-examine our bully voice, we're looking for evidence outside ourselves to see if what it's saying is actually true. Treat it as if it's the court of law. For instance, when I told myself that people liked me better if I drank, I could have played the role of prosecuting attorney and cross-examined that thought by considering the evidence. Did someone actually tell me that? Did I read it somewhere? Did I see it on TV? Are there any studies that prove it? Where is the evidence that this story is true? Challenging the thought by examining the evidence makes it clear that outside of my own mind, this thought is not true.

To take this a step further, here are some self-examination questions you can try:

1. Have I ever been in a situation where this belief was proven wrong?
2. What would I tell a friend who had this thought?
3. How does this belief make me feel, and is it helping me in any way?
4. What would happen if I chose to believe the opposite of what this voice is telling me?
5. What would change if I let go of these beliefs?
6. How does this story align with my values and the life I want to create?

Step 4. Let go of the old story

It took me a long time to realize the story I'd been telling myself for years. I never connected the belief that I wouldn't be loved and accepted unless I was perfect to the destructive choices and behaviors I made, especially with abusive eating and drinking. It wasn't until I got sober and worked with another woman in recovery, taking a hard look at my life on paper, that I began to recognize this damaging voice and actively work to change it. I became a woman with confidence and grace, capable of achieving anything I set my mind to. This included staying sober, caring for my physical body, rebuilding my life and career, and empowering other women to do the same, as you will learn more about in the following chapters.

Now that you may be more aware of your bully voice and the stories you have been telling yourself, it's time to set some intentions for some better-feeling thoughts. I invite you to challenge your old stories and the thoughts that go with them—literally—with a fun ritual inspired by *The Self-Care Oracle*, a deck created by Jill Pyle, CEO and Co-founder of Goddess Provisions. I've adapted this exercise and call it "The Bully Voice Exorcism."

Make sure you have a fire pit, fireplace, ashtray, or large bowl and somewhere safe to set fire to your bully voice. I usually go outside on my lanai and use the bowl where I keep my sage stick.

Take a few small sheets of paper and answer the following questions on each:

1. What stories about you, people, places, things, or experiences do you want to let go of?
2. What life experiences have you gone through or conquered that need to be acknowledged?
3. What specific thought patterns do you want to release?
4. What do you want to call in right now?
5. What desires do you want to manifest?

Set an intention to release and call in what you have written down by saying to the Universe, God, or your Higher Power of choice, "I release all negative thoughts and call in something better. And so, it is." Or you can make up something else that is more personal to you. Burn each piece of paper, and as you watch each piece burn, feel into it by envisioning yourself thriving in your new way of being, worry and stress-free. Imagine you are already that person you are calling in because you are actually already here.

Do this practice as often as needed. When you bring your attention to it, mindfully and intentionally release negative thought patterns, and call in what you desire, you are training your brain to default to more positive thoughts. This rewiring is known as Neuroplasticity.

Neuroplasticity simply refers to the brain's ability to reorganize itself by forming new neural connections in response to learning, experiences, and changes in the environment. The more you repeat a thought or behavior, the more you train your brain to create a new self-belief and habit. Repeating practices like this is a fun way to show yourself compassion and change the way you speak to yourself.

Step 5: Create your new story

Now that you've burned some of your negative thoughts with this last exercise and cleared space for more self-compassion and love, your new thoughts will influence you to take inspired action that will create more positive behaviors, healthier habits, and a belief in your highest self.

Take a moment to write your new story. For example, my new story became, *"I am perfectly imperfect, and that is enough. I am exactly where I am supposed to be at this very moment."* When I tell myself this, I feel less pressure to perform. I don't feel the need to compare myself to others. I feel grateful for what I've accomplished and embrace all that I am and have. These feelings build the momentum I need to keep moving forward in my own time to create the abundant life I desire.

Write your new story. Find creative ways to reinforce this story daily. Set it as wallpaper on your phone, set reminders with your Alexa device, put Post-it notes around your house, or add it to your vision board. Find what works for you and notice how it makes you feel and what different actions you take as a result. You can write your story in the space below.

My New Story

Download and print your Self-Healing Invitation here:

Mindset Is Everything

Our mindset shapes our outlook, behavior, and, ultimately, our path to personal abundance. Still, we need to pay attention to how we are treating ourselves, just as we did in the previous exercises. The awareness we cultivate from these mindfulness practices can unlock the door to profound transformation, allowing us to rewrite our story, break free from limiting beliefs, and step into a life of true fulfillment and purpose.

As Dr. Wayne Scott Anderson, one of the nation's foremost experts in nutritional intervention and lifestyle management, explains in *Dr. A's Habits of Health* (Dr. A's Habits of Health Press, 2019), "If we are not prepared to shift our mindset and focus on the necessary behavioral changes, then we're set up to struggle, fail, or quit."

Whether it's a program for nutrition, addiction, fitness, or any other transformation, starting with the right mindset is crucial. Without it, you're likely to abandon your efforts, leaving yourself vulnerable to self-criticism and falling out of alignment with your deepest desires and values. When you're out of alignment with the higher version of yourself, it's easy to slip back into a victim mentality, clinging to the old beliefs that whisper, "I can't. I'm not good enough. This is as good as it gets."

Cultivating mindfulness, challenging your bully voice, reframing your thoughts, and creating a new story can shift you from a limited belief mindset to a growth mindset, paving the way for true transformation. This shift sets you up for success by:

- **Boosting confidence:** A positive attitude strengthens your resilience, keeping you motivated and capable of overcoming obstacles.
- **Clarifying goals:** A focused mind helps you set clear, specific goals and pursue them with determination.
- **Enhancing problem-solving:** With a solution-oriented mindset, you approach challenges creatively and effectively.
- **Fostering adaptability:** A flexible mindset allows you to navigate change with ease, which is essential for lasting transformation.
- **Encouraging growth:** Embracing learning and personal growth becomes natural, fueling your journey to new skills and knowledge.

- **Building resilience:** A resilient mindset turns failures into learning experiences, keeping you moving forward.
- **Increasing productivity:** The right mindset enhances focus and productivity, helping you achieve your goals.
- **Strengthening relationships:** Positive thinking improves your interactions, leading to stronger support from others.
- **Taking informed risks:** A balanced mindset enables you to assess risks wisely, making better decisions on your path to success.

If you've experienced even the slightest shift in your perspective so far, you are shifting towards a growth mindset and are ready to take action in the rest of this book. You can always come back and revisit these exercises again and again, as mindset shifting is not a one-and-done experience. But it does have to happen first for the transformational process to begin. If you don't believe that change is possible for you, you won't experience change. If you're not *all in* and have doubts, transformation will take longer. It doesn't mean it can't happen, it just means you may not be ready right now, and that is perfectly OK. For now, know that mindset shift has the remarkable ability to reshape our reality, empowering us to thrive in any circumstance.

NOURISHING

HABITS

Chapter 6: Rest to Nourish

On this pathway to healing that I was creating for myself, I came to understand that nourishment encompasses more than just the intake of food and nutrients; it involves nurturing and sustaining various aspects of our well-being, including physical, mental, emotional, and spiritual dimensions. In the next three chapters, we'll explore rest, movement, nutrition, and how my perspective has shifted over time with respect to how each can be used to nourish us from the inside out.

When my lifestyle revolved around drinking, I couldn't tell you what being rested felt or even looked like. I lived every minute of the day with a hangover. I used alcohol not only to escape from what troubled me but to quell my anxiety, feel calm, and sleep. I thought my daily bottle of wine was helping. But it was actually causing a complete breakdown in my physical, emotional, and spiritual health.

For years I woke up with resentment. I resented the alarm clock that was forcing me out of bed. I resented having to make it through the next eight hours at my job with a hangover. I resented my co-workers for showing up energetic and smiling, ready for another day while I felt depressed and gross in my body. My excessive drinking late into the evenings left me feeling sluggish, bloated, and nauseated. It felt like having a flu bug every day, and over time, I just adapted to this feeling and settled for it as the best I was going to feel.

Even though for years I was unwilling to change, it was obvious to me that my daily drinking was the reason I felt this way. I chose the lifestyle that led me down a path of exhaustion and burnout. Once I got sober, it became clear to me that prioritizing rest, in addition to properly nourishing and hydrating myself, were essential steps toward healing physically and mentally. The lack of rest I was experiencing was a significant contributor to my cognitive decline, so once I was able to eliminate the alcohol, not only was I able to sleep much better, but I was able to start repairing the damage that I was doing to my brain and improve my cognitive functioning.

The Importance of Rest Periods

Sleep deprivation caused complete system shutdowns for me. I could not function well on any level. My productivity declined, my energy was sparse, my gut health was a mess, and I experienced constant heartburn and acid reflux. This made it difficult to digest my food properly and made me very sensitive to certain foods. Lack of sleep affected so many things, and it only made me feel more stressed. It was a vicious cycle that didn't stop until I stopped drinking.

Insomnia or poor sleep can also result from a health condition, a relationship or family crisis, grief, running on autopilot, constant worrying, or a myriad of other issues. As we work to resolve these life circumstances, rest becomes crucial to increase our mental stamina, strengthen our emotional resilience, and develop loving self-talk that is kind and gentle.

Many might think of rest as the act of sleeping, but we can give our bodies rest in a variety of ways, like short naps, for instance. I spoke to a friend recently who complained that she was only getting about three hours of sleep a night. Naturally, she always felt exhausted.

Averaging three hours of sleep per night was putting my friend at risk for developing health problems that could affect her cognitive function, immune system, blood pressure, weight, hormones, and insulin production. I suggested she start taking naps. At first, she resisted because she couldn't fall into a deep sleep during her naps, so it felt useless to her. But naps don't always require that we fall into a REM state, which is the deepest stage of sleep. You can benefit greatly from a 15 to 20-minute nap simply by resetting your system. This can give you a burst of alertness and increase motor performance. Emerging research shows that short naps can boost work productivity as well.

Short naps allow the body to get some light, restorative sleep that can enhance short-term memory and give your brain a quick refresh so you have the stamina for the remainder of the day. It's a mindfulness practice to allow ourselves to stop throughout the day and allow our minds and bodies to process, heal, and restore. Rest and mindfulness are connected because mindfulness encourages us to be fully present during periods of rest, enabling us to truly experience and appreciate the rejuvenating benefits of relaxation.

Giving ourselves this time outside of our sleeping hours can not only improve our sleep but can reduce stress, enhance mental clarity, boost energy, and increase our productivity.

Our days can pile up with activities that keep us on autopilot, and way too often, we don't stop at all to catch our breath. We move from one meeting to the next, drive our kids to sports, scramble to get dinner on the table, help the kids with their homework, finish our own work late into the night, try to keep up with our relationships, and maybe squeeze in a workout session. In between all of that, we don't even stop to just breathe. The next thing you know, we find ourselves grouchy, tired, frustrated, and moody. Our brains are wired, and our bodies are revved up well into the evening. By the time we go to bed, we haven't given ourselves an opportunity to wind down, so we either only get a few hours of sleep or we don't reach deep sleep, leaving us feeling tired the next day. It's a vicious cycle that leaves many of us feeling emotionally drained, burned out, and physically run down.

Resting should be deliberate, which means we are blocking out time in our day to break from our day to recharge, whether it's a brief walk, a short nap, listening to music, or stretching. Taking short rest periods throughout our day can benefit us in several ways:

1. **Stress reduction**: Short breaks allow us to step away from stressful tasks, reducing the accumulation of stress hormones like cortisol. This can help promote a sense of calm and relaxation.

2. **Improved focus and productivity**: Regular breaks prevent mental fatigue and boost concentration. When we return to work after a brief rest, our minds are refreshed and better able to focus on tasks.

3. **Enhanced creativity**: Rest periods provide an opportunity for our brains to process information and make new connections, leading to increased creativity and problem-solving abilities.

4. **Physical well-being**: Taking breaks encourages movement and reduces the negative effects of prolonged sitting or repetitive tasks. It can prevent physical strain and muscle tension.

5. **Mood improvement**: Rest releases feel-good hormones, like serotonin and endorphins, which play a key role in regulating mood and reducing stress.

6. **Better decision-making**: Rest helps us make more rational and effective decisions by preventing mental fatigue and allowing us to approach problems with clarity.

7. **Improved relationships**: Regular breaks can lead to better interactions with others by reducing irritability and promoting patience and empathy. An emotionally balanced state influences how we respond to others, allowing us time to pause before reacting and giving us space to show up with love and compassion.

We can incorporate rest in as little as 10 minutes a day, which makes it both beneficial and manageable when we're not used to giving ourselves this restorative time. If we can manage just a few 10-minute rest periods throughout the day, we can quickly build up to an hour or two, which helps us strike a healthy balance between normal daily stressors and relaxation.

However, rest periods can be as long as you need. The most important thing is to internationally schedule them in. Taking short rest periods can help us tap into our Third Eye Chakra, our innate wisdom, strengthening our intuition and creative thinking. This can be significant for someone who struggles with exhaustion or performance throughout the day.

As Alex Soojung-Kim Pang explains in *Rest*, "In our busy lives, we can't treat rest as something that we'll do when we've finished everything else. A block of time will never magically make itself available for rest. We have to make time for it."

I will admit, I was never a good example of giving myself rest periods throughout my day. I thought it was more about the number of sleeping hours than incorporating restorative time throughout my day until I read Pang's book. Prior to working from home in 2023, I had the kind of job where I was on my feet all day, client-facing, managing teams, and only getting a 30-minute break for lunch. I worked non-stop most days from 9:30 am until 6:30 pm with one break period. In addition to just being on my feet all day, I had to maintain mental toughness while interacting with so many different people and personalities, addressing various customer situations, coaching my team, and showing up as a leader for my own boss. I used to pride myself on my stamina, awarding myself with lazy evenings at home on the couch to survive another day. And this job wasn't easy. It was both physically and mentally draining, as well as stressful.

If I had been aware of why balancing rest and work throughout the day was so important for our overall well-being, I would have been practicing it. But it never crossed my mind until I read Pang's deeply insightful book.

When I started working from home as a full-time coach, I embraced the ability to incorporate rest periods throughout my day since my schedule was my own. But even then, I wasn't really doing it because it hadn't been a habit of mine. So, I started to strategically block time on my calendar for my downtime, even setting alarms or having my Alexa device remind me when it was time to stretch or meditate. This way, I could make sure I wasn't waiting until the end of the day to get my body and mind into a relaxed state necessary for a good night's sleep.

Another tool I started using to further cultivate my awareness around my rest and sleep is a health tracker ring, which is basically a wearable health device. The ring tracks sleep patterns, activity levels, heart rate, and body temperature. This data is then analyzed to provide insights into your overall health and help you optimize your daily habits for better well-being.

When I started using the ring, I was surprised at what I was learning. My stress levels seemed high, even when I wasn't feeling stressed, and I clearly was not giving my body enough restorative time. The device keeps track as the day progresses and makes recommendations on the App while educating on various health-related issues related to stress and rest. Having this data available has made me accountable for intentionally scheduling in restorative time so that it balances out my physiological stress. The data has also been helpful in how I perceive stress and rest. I no longer look at stress as the enemy but as a friend and fuel for a healthy lifestyle. It's my job to strike a balance between stress and rest and build the necessary healthy habits.

If I had this tool when I was working full time, I could have had more awareness of how being on my feet all day, with little to no breaks, was having an impact on my stress levels. Even if we have a job where our work hours are defined for us, we still have the freedom to take small breaks throughout the day. One of the best tools for reminding us to take a break is our own phones. We can set an alarm and then set a timer. We just need to be intentional about it.

Physiological stress is not bad stress. Rather, it's normal daily stress that we all experience. Things like exercise, socializing, coffee, and alcohol can all raise our physiological stress levels, but if we don't create balance, our stress levels can stay elevated and become chronic, therefore harmful to our health by interfering with our sleep. And if we're not getting quality sleep because we've had high stress levels all day, sleep deprivation will raise our cortisol levels and create even more stress, leading to decisions and behaviors that can be detrimental to our overall well-being. We'll take a look at some of these further in this chapter.

You don't need to go out and buy an expensive device to track your health, but it is a great tool to build awareness around this area of health. My hope is that by sharing my experiences, you will start bringing some mindfulness to the stress and rest in your own life. Paying attention to the cues from your body at certain times of the day, like brain fog or headaches, honoring what your body needs, like a nap or walk in nature, and creating your own habits, as a result, is a great starting point. Mindfulness is key here; without it, we could easily move like the energizer bunny all day without a second thought, and any opportunity for rest is lost.

Revisit the ten-minute mindfulness practices we covered in Chapter 3 to help you integrate rest into your day so you can reserve more energy, repair cell damage, and process and store memories. Since rest helps to boost your feel-good hormones, you'll naturally shift from a sympathetic nervous state to a parasympathetic state, which is the foundation for a quality night of sleep.

Sleep and Anxiety

Now that we understand physiological stress a bit more and that it is a short-term response to immediate challenges or threats, let's address a stress response that isn't so favorable. Anxiety.

Stress and anxiety are not one and the same. Anxiety, unlike physiological stress, is persistent and can linger even when there is no obvious reason for it. It is often a disproportionate reaction to perceived threats, causing ongoing worry and fear that disrupts daily functioning and can feel debilitating for some.

Anxiety is influenced by a combination of genetic factors and lifestyle habits. Although some are genetically predisposed and more susceptible to anxiety disorders, certain lifestyle habits can exacerbate anxiety symptoms, such as poor diet, substance use, lack of exercise, poor hydration, and lack of sleep. Let's look at sleep, specifically.

Persistent worrying and stress can activate the body's fight or flight response, releasing stress hormones like cortisol, which can interfere with the body's ability to relax and unwind at bedtime. Anxious thoughts that arise will keep the mind active, making it difficult to quiet it down. Anxiety can manifest physically, resulting in tension and discomfort that can make sleep difficult. Managing our stress throughout the day is crucial for quelling anxiety and developing good sleep habits. Without good sleep habits, we may find ourselves making unhealthy choices that end up discouraging quality sleep, leaving us feeling even more fatigued, cognitively impaired, moody, and physically unwell. These could look like:

1. Using sleeping pills or other substances to induce sleep, which can lead to dependency and worsen sleep quality over time.
2. Replacing alcohol with sugary treats like ice cream or candy. Eating these, especially late at night, can disrupt digestion and make it harder to fall asleep.
3. Relying on stimulants like caffeine late in the day to overcome fatigue from the night before. This can interfere with the ability to fall and stay asleep.
4. Prolonged periods of being sedentary can lead to increased levels of stress hormones, like cortisol, which can interfere with sleep onset and quality.

I had a tendency to bring stress upon myself, but my lifestyle habit of drinking created a vicious cycle of anxiety that prevented me from getting sufficient sleep for years. Drinking was my way of numbing stress, but it backfired by creating even more anxiety. Once I was in a chronic state it was really hard to get out of. Not drinking would have been a good idea, but since I wasn't ready to do that, I allowed the vicious cycle to continue for years.

How many times do you hear people proclaim how wonderfully they slept after a night of not drinking alcohol? For those who can drink in moderation, an early glass of wine is perfectly fine, and it may even be beneficial in some ways. But drinking alcohol late into the evenings is known to disrupt sleep. And for an alcoholic like me, who used it as a sleep aid, it severely affected my body's ability to experience all the necessary stages of sleep, including REM and deep sleep, which help us to create and store memories and repair and heal. Since my body was processing alcohol throughout the night, I would wake up multiple times and have trouble falling back to sleep, which caused more anxiety, resulting in fatigue, cognitive impairment, and mood disturbances. Over time, I could not function at a job, have an intelligent conversation, or muster up any kind of energy to engage in healthy movement.

This is an extreme case for an alcoholic like me, who deliberately used alcohol throughout the night to sleep. But for many moderate drinkers, alcohol can still disrupt sleep just enough to affect their performance levels the next day.

During the last year and a half of my drinking, I slept with a bottle of vodka underneath my pillow in case I woke up and couldn't fall back to sleep, which happened pretty much every night. The booze alleviated my anxiety which was keeping me awake, allowing me to slip back into restful unconsciousness, or so I thought. When I woke up in the morning, I needed another swig from the bottle just to get out of bed and not shake from DTs (delirium tremens). DTs are a severe type of ethanol withdrawal that can actually kill you if it's not monitored closely, and I experienced a milder type that progressed to more severe. Severe DTs can result in cardiovascular collapse, and there were many, many nights when I would go to bed after experiencing them, praying to God that I would wake up the next morning.

My need for alcohol progressed from a solution to ease my anxiety to being able to simply function. Once the disease progressed to a physical compulsion, I needed it to be able to get out of bed in the morning, walk to the coffee maker, and pour a cup of coffee without spilling it from all the shaking. It's what they call the "hair of the dog that bit you." Ingesting a small amount of alcohol temporarily eased the discomfort of a hangover. I wouldn't recommend it to anyone as a solution for a hangover, as it can lead to even more alcohol consumption. That was what it did for me, and before I knew it, I was intoxicated for 24 hours a day, even when I was sleeping.

I drank at work, in my car, and even when I babysat. I drank all day, every day, and was far from being rested and well-nourished.

I know many who aren't alcoholics drink in the evenings with the intention of winding down and falling asleep faster. There's nothing wrong with enjoying an evening cocktail in moderation if you don't struggle with alcohol addiction, but if it's used as a means to fall asleep, it ends up counteracting the good intention.

Drinking alcohol close to bedtime actually interferes with sleep and disrupts REM (rapid eye movement) sleep, which is crucial for cognitive function, memory consolidation, and emotional regulation. Alcohol can shorten REM sleep cycles and decrease the overall time spent in this restorative sleep stage, despite getting 7-8 hours of sleep. This interference can lead to fragmented sleep patterns and may contribute to feelings of grogginess, brain fog, and emotional imbalances the next day. This habit of drinking alcohol late into the evenings can exacerbate anxiety and ultimately lead to chronic stress, which negatively impacts energy levels, productivity, connections, and mood.

Once I got sober, my sleep issues weren't immediately resolved. My body took its time to repair itself with the help of mindset work, nutrition, and quality rest. I had to learn new sleep habits and understand that repairing the damage that lack of sleep had on me, inside and out, was going to take time.

In the beginning, my sleep cycle was a lot different from before because I was at the shelter. I would go to bed at 11 p.m. and wake up at 4:30 a.m. so I wouldn't miss out on the coffee in the morning. You'd think I would have a hard time sleeping in the same room with 20 other women, some who snored and some who tossed and turned. But somehow, I learned how to sleep again and felt more restored than I had in years.

I created a nighttime routine while I was there, one that I still use today. I actually grew to love getting in my bunk (I was on the top) well before I closed my eyes to get comfy and nestled in with a journal and book. I had a little window next to my bed, which rested right up against the wall, and I would look out at the stars and just breathe. I was happy not to be drunk and in trouble.

I would journal, writing down everything I was experiencing in this new life, and then escape with a book right before I closed my eyes. I remember feeling excited to get out of bed in the morning, even if it was 4:30 am. I'd sleep straight through the night and wake up excited for my coffee and morning routine. I'd read my daily inspiration from Melody Beattie's *Language of Letting Go* and journal on the daily reading. I'd sit somewhere quiet, away from everyone else, and just align.

My evening and morning routines helped me to feel rested and energized at their intended times, and when done daily, helped me to regain some balance mentally and be in the energy of anticipated excitement.

Benefits of Good Sleep Hygiene

One of the first things people say when they stop drinking is that they sleep better. This is true and is the first step, but in order to achieve optimal rest and sleep for the long term, we can't ignore the benefits of good sleep hygiene. This is the case for everyone, not just those recovering from alcohol abuse. Developing good sleeping habits can alleviate anxiety, no matter what we're healing from, by promoting a sense of calm and relaxation.

Long-term sleep deprivation can put us at risk for health problems involving our hormones, reproductive system, heart, metabolism, emotional response, respiratory system, and immune system. Getting adequate quality sleep can significantly improve brain performance, reduce stress hormones, enhance mood regulation, strengthen your immune system, heighten focus and creativity, and increase libido.

Self-Healing Invitation: Sleep Hygiene Assessment

Here are a few questions to ask yourself to check your own sleep hygiene. The insight you gain from your answers can help you get clear on what small changes you can make for improved sleep, if this is an area of struggle for you.

1. What time do you typically go to bed and wake up?

2. How many hours of sleep do you usually get per night?

3. Do you have a consistent bedtime routine? If so, what does it involve?

4. Are there any factors that tend to disrupt your sleep, such as noise, light, or temperature?

5. Do you consume caffeine, alcohol, or heavy meals close to bedtime?

6. How often do you use electronic devices (e.g., phone, computer, TV) before bedtime?

7. Do you experience difficulty falling asleep, staying asleep, or waking up too early?

8. Have you noticed any patterns or triggers for sleep disturbances, such as stress or anxiety?

9. Do you engage in any relaxation techniques before bedtime, such as meditation or deep breathing?

10. How do you feel upon waking up in the morning? Do you feel refreshed and well-rested or tired and groggy?

Download and print your Self-Healing Invitation here:

Let's be honest: Sleep can be extremely challenging due to the daily demands of work and family and the pressure to "do it all." These pressures can feel even more daunting when you're healing from something traumatic and trying to keep things simple and calm as you adapt to a new way of living.

When stress is high, quality sleep is usually the first thing to be compromised. And when we don't get sufficient sleep, it causes imbalances in one or more areas of our physical, emotional, and spiritual health. If you gave sleep a low score on the health wheel in Chapter 2, notice what other areas of the wheel were out of balance. Where else were there gaps between where you currently are and where you want to be? Is there a correlation between those areas of your health and your sleep?

Let's take a closer look at the areas of our health affected by sleep deprivation:

1. **Cognitive impairment:** Sleep deprivation can lead to decreased cognitive function, impaired memory, reduced focus, and slower reaction times.
2. **Physical health:** People who don't get sufficient rest put themselves at risk of getting sick often or developing chronic health conditions associated with any of the major systems of the body, such as diabetes, obesity, or pain.
3. **Mental health:** Lack of sleep can contribute to an increased risk of mood disorders such as depression and anxiety.
4. **Impaired performance:** Sleep loss can hinder performance in daily tasks, including work, driving, and studying. Sleep impairment has been compared to driving under the influence. Those who drive with severe sleep deprivation are as much of a risk on the road as someone with a .08 blood alcohol level. Reaction time is shorter, and attention and focus are affected, as are decision-making and judgment.
5. **Emotional regulation:** Insufficient sleep may lead to irritability, heightened emotional responses, and difficulty managing stress.

6. **Hormonal imbalance:** Sleep plays a crucial role in regulating hormones, and inadequate sleep can disrupt hormone levels, leading to various health issues.

7. **Increased accident risk:** Fatigue from lack of sleep can lead to a higher likelihood of accidents and injuries. Again, slower reaction times, spatial awareness, and coordination are affected.

Setting Yourself Up for Sleep Success

Here are some simple and natural things that I do that can help set you up for sleep success:

- **Create a sleep-friendly environment:** Your sleep environment plays a significant role in the quality of your rest. Choose soothing colors for the walls, pillows and bedding that make you feel calm, like light blue, gray, or sage. Ensure your bedroom is cool, quiet, and dark while sleeping. Use blackout curtains or an eye mask to block out light. Consider earplugs or a white noise machine to minimize noise disturbances.

- **Watch your diet and hydration:** Be mindful of what you consume before bedtime. Avoid heavy meals, caffeine, and large amounts of liquids close to bedtime, as they can interfere with sleep. Your body has to work all night digesting food if you eat too close to bedtime. Opt for light snacks if needed and ensure you stay hydrated throughout the day to avoid discomfort during the night.

- **Engage in regular exercise:** Regular physical activity can contribute to better sleep quality. Engage in moderate exercise during the day, but try to avoid intense workouts close to bedtime, as they can elevate your energy levels and make it harder to fall asleep. Find an exercise routine that works for you and aim for consistency. Gentle yoga is a great option for movement if the evenings are what is convenient for you.

- **Create a sleep-conducive bed:** Invest in a comfortable mattress, pillows, and bedding that support your sleep preferences.

Everyone has unique needs, so experiment with different pillow types or mattress firmness levels to find what works best for you. Ensure your sleep environment is clutter-free and conducive to relaxation. If you can handle it, remove any electronic device from the bedroom, including the television.

- **Nap early**: While short power naps can be beneficial, long or late-day naps can interfere with your ability to fall asleep at night. If you need to nap, aim for a short duration (10-20 minutes) and do so earlier in the day.

- **Establish a consistent bedtime routine**: Creating a regular sleep schedule is crucial for your body to establish a natural circadian rhythm. Aim to go to bed and wake up at the same time every day, even on weekends. This consistency will train your body to recognize when it's time to rest, promoting better sleep quality.

- **Wind down with a bedtime routine**: Engage in relaxing activities an hour before bed to signal to your body that it's time to sleep. Avoid stimulating screens, such as phones, tablets, or laptops, as the blue light emitted can disrupt your sleep patterns. Instead, opt for calming activities like reading a book, taking a warm bath, practicing mindfulness or meditation, or listening to soothing music. Consider a 15-minute Yin Yoga or Qigong practice.

- **Consult a healthcare professional if needed**: If you constantly struggle with sleep issues or suspect an underlying sleep disorder, it's advisable to consult a healthcare professional. They can evaluate your sleep patterns, provide guidance, and recommend further steps, such as a sleep study or personalized treatment options.

10-Minute Mindfulness Practices for Sleep

Now that we've looked at adding restful activities throughout the day and setting ourselves up for success for a good night's sleep with some effective natural strategies, let's take a look at some 10-minute mindfulness practices that we can do before bed to really prepare our minds and bodies for a quality night of sleep. Mindfulness practices can enhance sleep quality by further reducing stress, promoting relaxation, increasing body awareness, regulating sleep patterns, and reducing rumination. By incorporating mindfulness practices in the evenings, you can calm the mind, tune into bodily sensations, and create a more balanced mental state conducive to restful sleep. Consistent mindfulness practice can also foster a regular bedtime routine which can help you let go of worries or concerns that can keep you up at night.

Try establishing a consistent routine of winding down for a minimum of 10 minutes doing one or more of the following mindful activities at least one hour before shutting off the lights:

- **Stretching**—Gentle stretching can release tension in the body.
- **Meditation**—Short guided meditations are a great tool for easing you into sleep. Apps like Calm or Insight Timer offer a variety by topic, as well as soothing music or soundscapes to relax your mind. Do one in bed and you might fall asleep before it's over!
- **Mini facial**—Enjoy 10 minutes of indulgence with a face scrub, mask, or anti-aging skin treatment. Try products that use pure ingredients and essential oils. The aroma of the essential oils work to ease the body and mind.
- **Shower**—The warmth of a shower helps to relieve tension throughout the body.
- **Foot soak in Epsom salts**—A foot soak is a great grounding practice. Add your favorite essential oil for the ultimate spa experience. Follow up with a short foot massage with your favorite foot lotion.
- **Sipping herbal tea**—Feel your body shut down and melt with hot chamomile or valerian root tea. Both have sedative properties that naturally prepare your body for sleep.
- **Aromatherapy**—Diffuse calming essential oils by your bed or place a drop on your wrists or pillows. Pure therapeutic grade oils

actually work at the cellular level to promote healthy functioning of your body.

- **Read a book**—Escape into someone else's world. If possible, choose paper books over electronic versions. Slip under the covers and let go.
- **Journal**—Use your journal to release negative emotions or energy that no longer serves you, clearing space for a new day. Have gratitude in your heart? Spend 10 minutes writing about it.
- **Deep breathing**—Deep breathing can relax your body and mind. Inhale deeply through the nose, hold it for a few seconds, then exhale slowly out the mouth. Repeat until you feel any tension released from your body.
- **Pet your fur baby**—This is healing for both you and your pet. Sitting quietly and stroking a dog or cat's fur settles the nervous system and shifts you into a parasympathetic state.

Essential Oils for Rest and Emotional Balance

Essential oils have gained popularity for their potential therapeutic benefits, their anti-aging properties, and versatile uses. I started using essential oils for their emotional benefits and diffused them next to my bed at night to feel calm and at peace.

In 2017, I was introduced to a line of essential oils known for their purity, potency, and power in supporting our health. It was during Hurricane Irma. I was staying at my cousin's house on the east coast of Florida since my home on the west coast was getting hit by this Category 5 storm. My boyfriend at the time came with me, and let's just say our relationship was also at a Category 5. I had been an emotional mess for a while.

My cousin's boyfriend's family was also staying at the house. On the second night there, I was sitting in front of the TV in the corner of the couch, trying to hold back tears. I was scared about what was happening at home. Everyone was playing cards and having fun while I sat there moping until my cousin's boyfriend's mother came up to me and asked, "Would you like to try an oil?" All of a sudden, the tears stopped, and I looked at her with my eyes lit up. "Yes, please." I swear I could hear the sounds of a chorus singing praises of joy.

My cousins and I gathered in the spare bedroom and sat on the bed as we passed oils around, smelling them and rubbing them on our skin. We were given a short lesson on each oil as we passed it around, and I found myself amazed that they could be used for so many things like emotions, pain, digestion, immune strength, and sleep. Even more, there was a whole line of natural supplements made with oils that could be used to support every system in the body as well. I was intrigued. I hadn't realized that what I was using at home was actually toxic for my system and my environment and how much better I could support the health of my mind and body just by making these oils a daily habit. By the time we were done passing them around, I smelled like a tropical forest with oranges and eucalyptus plants. I was in heaven.

I left that weekend with oils in hand, ready to be a wellness advocate for this company. I had found something of my own that I was passionate about that would help me regain some emotional balance and possibly help others with their anxiety as well. Best of all, I was able to channel some of that anxious energy and put it to good use. I wanted to share the love with one person at a time, one oil at a time.

I went home and started experimenting and researching. I wanted to learn everything I could about these oils, including how to administer them, their wide range of benefits, what ailments they could be used for, their main constituents, top properties, and what they blended well with. I felt like a mad scientist coming up with various diffuser recipes that would enhance mood, induce sleep, boost creativity, or calm anxious feelings. The possibilities were endless.

Here are a few ways that I've found essential oils to be beneficial:

1. **Aromatherapy:** Essential oils can be used in aromatherapy, which involves inhaling the scents to promote relaxation, stress relief, and emotional well-being.
2. **Mood enhancement:** Certain essential oils, such as lavender or citrus oils, may help uplift your mood and create a more positive atmosphere.
3. **Natural remedies:** Pure essential oils have various properties that can support overall wellness. For example, tea tree oil may have antibacterial properties, while peppermint oil might help with digestion and headache relief.
4. **Personal care:** Essential oils can be used to create natural and personalized skincare products. They may offer benefits such as moisturizing, soothing, or revitalizing the skin.
5. **Cleaning and purifying:** Some essential oils possess antimicrobial properties and can be used in natural cleaning products. They can help freshen the air, eliminate odors, and maintain a clean environment.

I soon found myself swapping out my skincare, cleaning supplies, candles, perfumes, and home fragrances for these essential oils, understanding that they are about more than their pleasant smell. They are a tool that I use to ensure that I am using the cleanest, purest, most health-beneficial ingredients in my system whenever possible. I could write a whole book on the topic, but right now, I want to address how the oils helped me with my anxiety and my sleep.

The number one reason we are restless and can't sleep is because we are stressed! We all experience it. We all have it from time to time, some more severe than others. Just to recap, stress can significantly impact our health by triggering a cascade of physiological responses. When stress becomes chronic, it can lead to imbalances in hormones such as cortisol, affecting various bodily functions. This sustained elevation of stress hormones may contribute to issues like high blood pressure, weakened immune systems, and disrupted sleep patterns. Additionally, chronic stress can influence behaviors like overeating or adopting unhealthy coping mechanisms, further exacerbating health problems. While stress is not necessarily the root of all health issues, it can be a significant contributing factor. When stress prevents us from getting adequate rest, it can impede our ability to function optimally.

Even one night with less than seven hours of sleep makes me feel like I have a hangover the next day, and I will tell you that I did not get sober to have hangovers from lack of sleep! I get nauseous, my digestive system doesn't function properly, I can't focus on my work, and I tend not to get much done. I get moody and irritable and make poor food choices, all from one lousy night's sleep.

When I found my oils, that changed. Pure essential oils can help improve sleep and relaxation through the mechanisms we mentioned above. Scents like lavender, chamomile, or bergamot are known for their soothing properties. When inhaled, they can influence the limbic system, the part of the brain associated with emotions and memories.

Let me share some of the science behind the oils that I have learned in my training. Incorporating essential oils into your daily routine can promote relaxation at the cellular level. At the cellular level, the effects of pure essential oils are often attributed to their bioactive compounds. They contain various molecules, such as terpenes and phenols that can interact with the cells and biochemical processes. When inhaled or applied topically, these compounds may enter the bloodstream and reach different cells and tissues, providing a natural solution to support various health issues. Oils like lavender, for example, have been studied for their potential to influence neurotransmitters, such as promoting the release of calming neurotransmitters like serotonin. Others, like chamomile, may interact with receptors in the brain associated with relaxation.

Unless you are an essential oil enthusiast, you probably wouldn't know this and simply associate essential oils with their soothing aromas, which naturally help us to feel relaxed. But as you can see, the benefits extend far beyond their pleasant smell. It's important to invest in 100% pure therapeutic-grade oils to get these kinds of benefits. If they haven't been tested for purity, and if you don't know where they are sourced from, you don't really know what you are getting. Also, there are many oils out there that you can buy off the shelf where the purity is compromised by being adulterated.

Investing in just one or two oils can go a long way in supporting your overall well-being and can be a very helpful natural solution to help you feel more rested. Using oils throughout the day and then with your evening routine, or just simply diffusing next to your bed, can help prepare your mind and body for rest. Coupled with a mindfulness practice like meditation, journaling, or reading can really enhance your overall experience.

Have some fun and create your own winding-down ritual. I've given you a lot of examples of how you can set your body and mind up for better sleep, so challenge yourself for the next few weeks and establish your new evening routine.

By implementing some simple strategies and making sleep a priority in your life, you can enhance the quality of your rest and enjoy the numerous benefits of a rejuvenated mind and body. Remember, everyone's sleep needs are unique, so be patient and allow yourself time to find the routine and habits that work best for you. Sleep well and wake up ready to conquer the day!

Learn more about the health benefits of implementing an essential oil routine.

Chapter 7: Move to Nourish

I've always been active. My parents always kept my brothers and I engaged in some kind of sport growing up. They started us with swimming, tennis, and skiing. Then, my brothers moved on to baseball and football while I tried dance. I was never a good dancer. I was clumsy and awkward, and was always in the back row during recitals since I was the tallest girl in the group. Let's just say dance and I weren't a good fit.

I quit dancing after the eighth grade and focused on my tennis game. Up to this point, my parents had sent me to tennis camp every year, and I had a personal coach. He used to get so mad at me for my attitude during practices. I would be so hard on myself when I wasn't playing well, and I'd just want to "throw in the racquet." I'd mope, stomp, and slap my racquet against things—I acted like such a brat. I could never just enjoy myself in the game. Every bit of it was about winning, and I was *not* a fan of being a competitor.

In high school, I joined the tennis team. I spent freshman year on the junior varsity team as a top singles player, then moved up to varsity my sophomore year and played doubles. I became one of the team captains in junior year alongside my good friend, and the two of us competed for two years for the number one singles spot. I spent half the season senior year in the number one spot until she kicked my butt and moved me down to second. The defeat was hard for me, but I had an undefeated record as the second-best player on the team, which eased my frustration.

I never thought of tennis as something I could just play and enjoy. It was only about winning, so naturally, I stopped playing after high school. If I couldn't be the best, I didn't want to participate because my bully voice always told me that if I wasn't the best, I wasn't good enough. I felt this way about many things—getting the lead in the school play, landing the solo in the choir, graduating at the top of my class, and even returning to school with a better tan than my friends after the summer break. I had a serious case of unworthiness unless I was on top.

It wasn't until after my last tennis season in the fall of senior year that my disordered eating started. At that point, in the dead of winter, I started my own exercise routine at home with the intention of losing weight. I didn't enjoy it. In fact, I dreaded getting on that stationary bike in the cold, damp basement where my mom did the laundry. I ran sprints up and down the basement stairs until I was exhausted and sweaty; I did multiple sets of crunches and sit-ups. To me, exercise was for the sole purpose of shedding weight. In a way, I abused it, exercising excessively. It didn't give me pleasure. I didn't notice the endorphins. The only goal was to be thin.

No one ever questioned what I was doing or why. They didn't even catch onto the fact that I was losing weight because, at that time, I could hide under my oversized sweaters. Once summer came and it was bathing suit weather, it was hard to hide my protruding bones, and my eating and excessive exercise became suspicious to my parents. This was when my dad put me on the scale for the first time, and I got grounded for being too thin.

The day he made me weigh myself should have been one of the happiest days for me. I got accepted into college that day, but instead of celebrating, I got punished. I had been with a friend that day down at my beach house, and when we got home, it was revealed to my parents that I hadn't eaten all day. That was all it took for my dad to throw me on the scale.

My basement workout sessions came to an end. I was off to college soon after that, and I had lost quite a bit of weight, so it didn't bother me. I welcomed the break from that dingy basement. Through the rest of the summer, I'd continue counting calories, though.

Once I was in college, movement became more about keeping the weight off. I started going to the university gym during my freshman year to make sure I avoided that 'freshman 15' everyone was always talking about. Let's just say it didn't work because, somehow, I had gained a good 10 pounds during my first semester. I noticed the weight gain when I was home for winter break that year, so I got back on board with a very restrictive diet, skipping meals and counting calories, and made sure to burn off every single one on the stair machine.

Then I discovered long-distance running.

The first time I ran long distance was during Greek Week during my sophomore year. My friend and I volunteered to represent our sorority and run the three-mile challenge. I didn't have proper running shoes, and my friend always suffered from shin splints, so I don't quite remember what enticed us to participate. All I know is that from that day forward, I never stopped running.

I remember how good it felt to be out on the trail, with the leaves crunching under my feet, not really knowing where the trail would lead me. The sun was shining, and the temperature was a perfect 75 degrees. It was an escape from the stress of exams and final projects. It was a moment where I could take pressure off myself and just move freely. It was liberating.

I loved not having to go to the gym to exercise. Running gave me all the cardio workout I needed. It gave me a different kind of endorphin rush, the kind that made me feel powerful and in control. My muscles had a slight ache when I was done, which felt deliciously rewarding.

But as wonderful as the experience was of being outside and connecting with nature, I lost sight of that connection for a period of time as I became more and more obsessed with running just to burn calories. Although I was still experiencing the endorphin rush from a good four-mile run, I didn't necessarily enjoy the run itself. It felt more like a chore, a chore that helped me shed pounds once again. I became addicted and felt guilty for taking a day off.

After graduating college, I worked in New York City. It was an hour's commute from New Jersey, where I was living. This meant getting up at 5:00 a.m. to get my daily run in before I caught the train into Hoboken. It was my sacred time and how I learned to connect my mind with my body again. My running became more of a way to nourish myself from the inside out instead of a tool to stay thin.

I worked with a group of people whose idea of work-life balance was to work, work, and work more. There was a lot of pressure and really late nights at the office. Running was one thing I could do to stay sane. It was a time when no one had access to me. It was a space where chaos was not welcome, only serenity. It was how I built resilience and mental toughness. It was how I meditated and how I was able to keep calm for the rest of the day, even if I had a 15-hour day at the office.

Running outside not only nourished my body with the energy I needed to get through long days, but it fueled my mind with better-feeling thoughts that helped me power through the verbal abuse, work pressures, and toxic flow that ran through the office. I eventually quit that job, feeling completely misaligned with that whole culture, and went back to school to earn my master's degree in Writing and Publishing. And, of course, my running went with me.

Being sedentary was never an option for me. Even though I abused my body with it for a period of time, I'm grateful my parents had me physically active as a child. Growing up, I didn't sit in front of television sets or play video games. We were always outdoors running, riding bikes, climbing trees, and playing all kinds of games with the neighborhood kids. Finding ways to move my body was a lifestyle my parents chose for me and one I chose to continue into my adult years. When I learned to love movement for the benefits outside of my physical appearance, I was able to approach it in a healthier way. And when I found running, I found my bliss. I could run without being competitive, and I could do it while being in my favorite place—outside in nature.

Movement has kept me healthy in my mind and my body and has always been a natural way for me to quiet my anxious thoughts, feel empowered, enhance productivity, and boost my mood. A sedentary lifestyle offers no health benefits unless you are recovering from an illness. Inactivity can lead to various health consequences, such as heart disease, obesity, and diabetes. Unpleasant side effects can include muscle weakness, decreased flexibility, weight gain, and difficulty sleeping.

Let's look at some of the physical and mental benefits of implementing movement into our day, even if it's just 10 minutes at a time.

Physical Benefits:

1. **Improved cardiovascular health:** Regular exercise strengthens the heart and enhances blood circulation, potentially reducing the risk of heart disease and high blood pressure.
2. **Weight management:** Exercise helps to burn calories and maintain a healthy weight, reducing the risk of obesity and related health issues.
3. **Increased muscle strength and endurance:** Engaging in strength training and resistance exercises can improve muscle tone, strength, and endurance.
4. **Enhanced flexibility:** Stretching exercises like yoga or Pilates can improve flexibility and reduce the risk of injuries.
5. **Better bone health:** Weight-bearing exercises contribute to stronger bones and reduce the risk of osteoporosis.
6. **Boosted immune system:** Regular physical activity can enhance the immune system's functioning, making it more efficient in fighting off infections and illnesses.

Mental Benefits:

1. **Reduced stress and anxiety:** Exercise stimulates the release of endorphins, which act as natural stress and anxiety relievers, promoting a more positive mood.
2. **Improved cognitive function:** Physical activity has been linked to enhanced cognitive abilities, such as better memory, attention, and problem-solving skills.
3. **Enhanced sleep quality:** Regular exercise can improve sleep patterns, leading to more restful and rejuvenating sleep.
4. **Increased self-esteem and body image:** Exercise contributes to a sense of accomplishment, boosting self-esteem, and promoting a positive body image.

Movement enhances the mind-body connection by improving physical health, which in turn boosts mental well-being and cognitive function. This interplay fosters better emotional regulation, stress reduction, and overall life satisfaction.

If exercise is not currently a part of your lifestyle, jumping into a rigorous fitness class or going for a four-mile run might just result in you being turned off by it or not wanting to try it again. Instead, start small. Adding 10 minutes of movement to your day is a great place to get started, and then you can build from there.

Here are ten ideas you can try:

1. **Quick high-intensity interval training (HIIT) workout:** Perform a series of bodyweight exercises like jumping jacks, burpees, and mountain climbers in short bursts with brief rests in between.
2. **Brisk walk or jog:** Go for a brisk walk or light jog around your neighborhood or a nearby park.
3. **Dance session:** Turn up your favorite music and have a fun dance session in your living room or, even better, in your bedroom in front of a mirror.

4. **Stair climbing:** If you have stairs at home or nearby, climb up and down for a quick cardiovascular workout.

5. **Tabata:** Try a Tabata workout, which involves doing one exercise intensely for 20 seconds, followed by 10 seconds of rest. Repeat this cycle for four minutes.

6. **Stretching routine:** Spend 10 minutes stretching various muscle groups to improve flexibility and relieve tension.

7. **Jump rope:** Jump rope for a few minutes to get your heart rate up and engage your whole body.

8. **Bodyweight circuit:** Create a circuit of bodyweight exercises like squats, lunges, push-ups, and planks, performing each exercise for one minute before moving on to the next.

9. **Hula hooping:** Grab a hula hoop and have some fun while working on your core muscles.

10. **Yoga flow:** Follow a short yoga flow sequence to promote relaxation, flexibility, and mindfulness.

Movement With Mindfulness

Mindfulness movement can turn us off autopilot and help to slow us down. Practices like yoga, Tai Chi, and mindfulness walking are excellent examples of movement that foster a strong mind-body connection because they focus our awareness on our body, breath, and surroundings.

The first time I experienced this mind-body connection with movement was on my bike all those years ago, as I described earlier in this book. Then in 2014, I tried yoga for the first time. I didn't know a thing about the practice, but I had been looking for something where I could work on my flexibility and muscle definition. Yoga gave me more than that. Gentle flow classes became my favorite type of practice because they taught me to slow down and breathe, which helped me with anxious feelings and overreacting. I wasn't aware of my breathing before I took yoga. My classes taught me how to connect each movement with a breath, which kept me focused on the present moment.

Yoga is my favorite mindfulness practice and one of the only places where I can be fully in the moment for an entire hour. When thoughts come in, which they do, I have the teacher's voice guiding me through the poses with emphasis on the breath. When I'm on my mat, I feel safe and anchored to the ground beneath me. I feel strong and secure, like Aladdin when he's on his magic carpet. When I'm on my mat, I'm on a journey, and nothing that is off the mat matters. Nothing else can access me. I am free.

The practice of yoga has helped me to heighten my awareness of how I feel in my body. The flow sequences help me to reduce my stress, improve my focus, and enhance my form and technique. I carry myself differently since starting yoga, with an awareness of my posture and the pace at which I walk. I've become more attuned to the physical sensations in my body, which has helped me to be more conscientious when making decisions and in how I respond to others.

A Beginner's Mind

If yoga isn't for you, there are so many other ways to bring mindfulness movement into your daily life and receive similar benefits. We can take the core principles of yoga and apply it to other types of movement, like stretching, walking, Tai Chi, or qigong. I like to take this mindfulness practice of connecting my breath with movement out to the lake behind my home.

Being out in nature is always a great place to get mindful. We can tap into all of our senses, like the feel of our feet in the grass, the sounds of birds, the shapes of the clouds, the colors in the sky after a sunset, smells in the air, or just the peace from the stillness. When I was drinking, I didn't notice anything. It was like walking through life blind. Today I can bring my awareness to my surroundings, noticing so many wonderful things. Just the other day, I stopped to watch a bald eagle. It was simply magnificent.

I take time to stop and watch a family of ducks sitting on the lake's edge and how the male and female mallards never leave each other's sides. I talk to the clan of turtles that swim over by the small bridge. When they see me coming, they think I have food, so they all swim up together, looking up at me as if to say, "Well, where's my snack?" I always get a kick out of how the baby turtles ride on the mother turtles' backs. There are just so many things to take notice of, and they bring a warmness to my heart.

My mindfulness walks outside are also a time to feel inspired, get creative, build momentum, and enliven my spirit. But it's important not to put pressure on ourselves if we're trying to get some kind of result out of it, like a divine download or our next big idea. In moments like this, it's important to just remember the foundational attitudes of mindfulness:

- A beginner's mind
- Acceptance
- Non-judgment
- Non-striving
- Letting go/letting be
- Patience
- Trust
- Gratitude and generosity

A beginner's mind opens us up to have a new experience each time, while acceptance allows us to be as we are in that moment. So, if we're especially tired on a walk or in our yoga practice, just accepting our current state will enable us to have the experience we are meant to have without judging ourselves or our performance. Non-striving is simply not reaching or chasing a certain result. Instead, we give ourselves permission to just be open to receive the benefits from our practice and let go of any expectations. Having patience through practice and trusting in the process leads us to a place of gratitude for giving ourselves the space and time to show ourselves this act of love, kindness, and compassion.

Mindfulness Movement Benefits

Practicing mindfulness during our movement activities can uplevel the benefits we get from just going through the motions. Specifically, mindfulness movement can:

1. **Enhance awareness:** Mindfulness helps you tune into your body and emotions during exercise, allowing you to better understand your limitations and strengths.
2. **Reduce stress:** Practicing mindfulness during workouts can reduce stress and anxiety, promoting a more relaxed and enjoyable experience.
3. **Improve focus:** It can boost your concentration, helping you stay present in the moment and make the most out of your workouts.
4. **Better form and technique:** Mindfulness can lead to better form and technique, reducing the risk of injury and improving the effectiveness of your exercises.
5. **Increase motivation:** By staying mindful, you can maintain motivation and stay committed to your exercise routine.

Self-Healing Invitation: Mindfulness Walking

I invite you to practice the walking meditation located on the resource page. You will also find a variety of mindfulness meditations to try here.

Now that we understand more about the holistic health benefits of mindfulness movement, let's explore mindfulness eating. This practice helped me to change my relationship with food and heal from my self-sabotaging eating patterns.

Chapter 8: Eat to Nourish

Nourishing our bodies is an act of self-love. Depriving ourselves of proper nourishment is an act of self-neglect.

I talked a bit about my struggle with an eating disorder that started in high school, and how I thought food was the enemy. When I made the decision to drastically cut calories, I eliminated experiences that once gave me joy, like my Sunday morning adventures with my dad. He and I would go to the bakery every Sunday after church to pick out rugelach, brownies and pastries together, and then we would head to the cheese shop, where we'd laugh and taste cheeses and pieces of bread. We had a favorite cheese we called "feet cheese," because it stank like feet but tasted so delicious. It was a special time spent with my dad every week, and I took it away from both of us.

The relationship I had with food reflected the relationship I had with myself. I loathed everything about my body, so I starved it. I despised myself so much that I refused to nourish myself, and as a result, I experienced both physical and emotional pain that lasted for years. I developed a spastic esophagus from all of the acid reflux, and I always felt nauseated. My doctor put me on a prescription medication so that I wouldn't develop an ulcer and could at least eat without all the heartburn. It became quite difficult to stomach certain foods, but I didn't mind. I didn't want to eat anyway. I became so dehydrated that my skin turned sallow in color, and my hair started falling out.

I felt so alone living with my secret of not eating. I'd lie to my parents, telling them I'd eaten when I hadn't, or insist on making my own dinner so I could secretly count calories. I told them I didn't eat red meat anymore, so I wouldn't have to eat what my mom had made. I'd witness everyone enjoying cakes and cookies during the holidays while I sat on the other side of the room, hoping no one would ask me why I wasn't having any. Not eating was hard work, but keeping it a secret was even more difficult.

This self-sabotage, this form of punishment, was a response to my belief that I wasn't good enough. The belief made me anxious and sad, so I chose to take the action of not eating to feel better. This action became my way of life for a long time.

There are plenty of other ways we can self-sabotage using food when we want to comfort ourselves from emotional pain. There are emotional eaters, binge eaters, crash dieters, and even those who will cook for everyone else, then watch them eat. Food becomes more of a harmful tool than a means to nourish, and it can throw us off balance with other areas of our well-being, like our sleep, mood, and relationships.

My unhealthy relationship with food kept me withdrawn. Once my friends and family were onto me, they told me my personality had changed. I didn't laugh or have fun anymore. I was intense and serious about everything, and I took everything personally. I wasn't a joy to be around anymore. That made me sad, but it didn't stop me. This addiction to not eating progressed into an obsessiveness that engulfed me. It was all I could think about, and it used up all of my mental energy.

When I was in college, I started binging and purging. I couldn't take the deprivation anymore, so I allowed myself to indulge in food again. I did further damage to my esophagus and developed a throat ulcer that felt like a golf ball stuck in my throat.

I remember feeling emotionally satisfied yet physically uncomfortable after a purge. Mentally, I was relieved to get rid of the bloating in my belly, but the cycle of binging and purging was exhausting. My throat would be sore and swollen, I'd have gastrointestinal discomfort, and the stomach acid would make my breath unbearable. I felt battered each time I did it, but to me, it was worth it to feel better about myself on the outside. I assumed I would be able to stop this self-destructive behavior whenever I wanted, but the physical act of throwing up over and over again made it very difficult for food to stay down. The guilt and shame were overwhelming, and I became disgusted with myself. I didn't ask for help because I was afraid of being controlled by someone else, like being watched all the time or told what to eat. What would they think of me? What if they couldn't accept this about me? I kept the secret to myself and suffered in silence.

I was living in a sorority house when I was at my worst with the binging and purging. Everyone knew about it, but no one said anything. I later found out that the girls on my floor could hear me throwing up behind my bedroom door. When I disposed of the evidence in the garbage cans outside my room, it produced a foul smell that everyone noticed in the hallway.

There were girls in the house who I always felt were leering at me. It became uncomfortable for me to eat with them in the dining room, so I'd go to the frozen yogurt stand because they sold non-fat yogurt, and it was an easy way for me to manage my calories in private. I started hibernating because I felt extremely insecure and uncomfortable in my skin. I didn't feel like myself anymore. I had always been a sociable, playful, and vivacious girl, but the shame, guilt and fear I felt left me feeling so small. It just felt safer to isolate in my room.

When I went home for Christmas break my senior year, my parents immediately noticed how thin I had gotten again. My dad stood in the kitchen and looked me up and down with this look of disgust on his face as if to say, *"Here we go again."* My parents were making dinner together like they normally did, something to celebrate my coming home. But it wasn't the happy homecoming I was hoping for. I couldn't care less about eating, and it showed. My dad was so pissed off at me that he had me get on the scale once again. My mom just allowed this because my dad made the rules, and the rule was that if I didn't start putting on weight, they would take me out of college. This ultimatum felt paralyzing.

I was scared of the thought of gaining weight. I agonized over this while I was home and felt uncomfortable in my parents' presence, as if every time they looked at me, they were judging me. That bully voice would say, *"Ya see? You don't look good enough for them, so now they're going to punish you and take you out of college."*

My one older brother was always my biggest fan, and he sat me down and had a heart-to-heart. I don't remember exactly what he said, but his words were full of compassion. There was no judgment but encouragement and love. He reminded me that I had too much going for me to screw it up just to be skinny. I agreed and we hugged. I felt so seen and loved, and I sat with his words while I was home and decided I wasn't about to trade in a college degree to be super skinny. After my relentless mission to be thin, I surrendered and admitted I needed to change. I'm grateful for that talk with my brother. There was something about it that struck me with the awareness of what I was doing to myself and how I was ruining my future. I was finally able to see my parents' point of view and understood why they were so concerned.

The surrender was easy. The healing process was not. My recovery took years, and later in my life, I learned the same thing about my alcoholism. My thinking and behaviors around my addiction to being thin and my addiction to alcohol were literally the same. I used each to change how I felt, to feel in control, and to be loved and appreciated by others.

When I returned for my second-semester senior year, I got to work on my relationship with food. Over time, I shifted how I felt about food by doing a few simple things.

1. I got super intentional with food.
2. I mentally prepared for food.
3. I remained open to food.

I became very intentional when it came to shopping, preparing, and eating my meals. Each week, I would pick out a few recipes to make since I was living in an apartment off campus, and I would carefully craft a shopping list before going to the store so I wouldn't spend time scrutinizing every nutrition label. I kept my meals simple so I didn't feel overwhelmed and found foods I loved that I looked forward to eating.

I thrived on routine, even back then. Each day, I'd go to my morning classes, go for my daily run, and then refuel with a turkey sandwich on whole wheat bread with Dijon mustard, mayo, tomato, and lettuce. I made my sandwich just the way I liked it and started looking forward to it each day. Following this routine day in and day out helped my brain to reorganize itself and form new neural pathways, rewiring the way I thought about food. I started to see food as a natural medicine and nourishment that was helping me to heal from food-related trauma.

I'd use a similar routine for dinner. I'd eat at the same time each day and spend time in my little apartment kitchen prepping, cutting up vegetables, assembling salads, and eating a well-balanced meal. I'd practice mindfulness eating, savoring each bite and noticing the textures, flavors, and smells. I'd focus on chewing and swallowing slowly, listening for the cues that my body was full. This was very important because the physical sensations from eating too fast or too much at one time could trigger me to want to purge again. So, mindful eating became extremely important in my healing journey.

This may or may not be for you, but if working on your relationship with food is an area you'd like to focus on, I am offering a few suggestions to get started. By no means do you have to have an eating disorder like I had to explore options for healthier eating. Making healthy choices when it comes to food benefits everyone. Food is how we feed our brain and body the fuel it needs to operate. Think of it like putting gas in your car. Your car can't run without it, and the better the gas, the better your car will operate.

1. **First, make the decision to work on your relationship with food.** If you can acknowledge that it is affecting the other aspects of your health—emotional, physical, social, and spiritual—commit to making some changes.

2. **Keep a food diary and record what, when, and why you eat.** Notice how you feel when you eat. What emotions come up? Who do you eat with? What kinds of choices are you making? Get it all down; the more, the better.

3. **Journal daily** to see if you can identify any patterns of negative self-talk or self-sabotage related to food.

4. **Commit to some kind of spiritual practice.** It could be meditation, nature walks, journaling, church, or other religious gatherings. Just do something so you can start connecting with a power greater than yourself to help guide you.

5. **Slowly incorporate some healthier options into your diet.** If you already do, then great. If you don't, then I've listed some general guidelines below.

6. **Always discuss this with your doctor.** If an eating disorder is recognized, they may suggest professional help. Don't overlook the help of a licensed nutritionist as well. You and your doctor can explore the nature of your relationship with food and the proper course of action to take.

Now that you've made a decision to work on your relationship with food, how do you go about making better decisions? Here are a few general guidelines if you don't have food restrictions. There's no need to get fancy. Just stick with some basic universal guidelines on healthy, balanced nourishment:

1. Focus on eating more whole foods, fruits, and vegetables.
2. Eat a balance of macros—carbohydrates, proteins, and healthy fats.
3. Try to eat less red meat and more lean poultry like chicken and fish.
4. Cut back on sugar, alcohol, and processed foods.

5. Drink eight 8 oz glasses of water daily.
6. Sleep 7-9 hours each night.
7. Move your body for 30 minutes a day or in multiple 10-minute increments.
8. Explore necessary supplements with your doctor.

I am not a nutritionist, so I won't make specific recommendations for eating plans, but this universal list is a starting point and gives you the opportunity to explore each item on its own. As discussed in the chapters prior, we can't overlook rest and movement when we're considering how we are nourishing ourselves. Food, rest, and exercise are interconnected, and how we sleep and move our bodies will strongly influence our decision-making about the foods we eat.

Making a few small shifts at a time, like adding more fruit and vegetables to your meals, will feel much more manageable than trying to overhaul your whole diet all at once. Each step creates awareness that will help you stay aligned with your endgame, whatever you choose that to be. As you become more aware, you'll be able to catch yourself before making a decision that may not be in your best interest. As you put this action on repeat, you'll create new habits that will motivate you to take another step towards healthier eating. Before you know it, you will have created a healthier lifestyle simply by making a few shifts at a time.

When I shifted my thoughts about food as something that would nourish me rather than harm me and implemented my new habits over time, I started noticing how much better I felt mentally and physically. Food was supplying me with the nutrients I was starving for and put the glow back into my face. Everything about my physical appearance started improving, like my hair, skin, and nails. I had color back in my face. I smiled more, and people noticed. This just fueled me to keep going. I felt good about how I was taking care of myself instead of guilty and ashamed of how I was treating my body. I started looking at the act of eating in a whole new way, as an act of self-love that was nourishing me from the inside out.

Here are some ideas I've used that help me to stay on track:

- **Explore your local farmer's market for your produce.** Most cities will have local markets where the fruits and vegetables are grown locally. When you buy produce that is grown locally, there is less chance that it is contaminated with chemicals because there is little transport time from farm to market. Shopping at farmer's markets is fun, gets you outside in the fresh air, connects you with the community, and can actually save you money.

- **Shop the perimeter of the grocery store.** The middle of the grocery store is where most of the processed foods live. Although it is hard not to buy something that is packaged, try to buy less, and remember that if it has a long shelf life, there are preservatives in it. If you can't refrain from shopping in the middle of the store, just take some extra time to examine labels and price per unit.

- **When buying something packaged, study the list of ingredients.** Can't decide? A good rule of thumb is that less ingredients are always better. For example, I love almond milk, but there are brands that add ingredients that I don't even understand. So, I opt for almond milk with three simple ingredients: filtered water, organic almonds, and sea salt. I know what I'm getting, and it takes the hard decision-making out of it. If there is something on the list you don't recognize, Google it.

- **Do your homework.** Research options, learn about ingredients, and Google search for the best alternatives if you're looking to make a switch. Just keep it simple. The less complicated you make it, the more time you can spend enjoying your healthy choices rather than stressing over making them.

- **Take an inventory of your refrigerator and pantry and do a weekly purge.** Clear space and make room for the healthier items. If your pantry is full of processed food, you're less likely to fill it with healthier alternatives like oats, nuts, and legumes. Start with one shelf if it feels too overwhelming, or a shelf that holds all your condiments. Take baby steps instead of doing a mass purge and replace.

- **Explore fresh and pure alternatives to add flavor to your dishes.** The fun thing about healthy eating is that there are so many options to jazz dishes up with natural ingredients. Default to using fresh herbs for a burst of flavor instead of using a lot of unnecessary fats and salty condiments. I love experimenting with fresh pressed olive oils and vinegars on my salads and pastas instead of buying bottled from the grocery store. I may spend a little more, but the fresh taste is worth it, and a little goes a long way.

- **Practice mindfulness throughout your day, especially when it comes to food.** Focusing on the moment you are in with food will create greater awareness of your thoughts, feelings, sensations, and reactions. It's this conscious awareness that we bring to our choices around food that can serve our health in a positive way. When we make good nutritional choices, we raise our vibe and build momentum around a healthy, nourishing mindset.

Mindfulness eating creates a space of time for us to cultivate self-awareness. It's a practice of slowing down, honoring the present moment, and tuning in to all of the sensations that arise when eating, such as the smells, the textures, the taste, and the visual appeal. In this moment of self-awareness, we help our minds and bodies relax and flow with ease. Mindfulness eating is considered a form of meditation that calms the nervous system, aids in digestion, and supports quality sleep. It's an act of appreciation and self-love.

Shawngela Pierce, who leads spiritual retreats in Sedona, Arizona, explains in an interview with *Natural Awakenings* (Collier/Lee Edition, September 2023), "When we slow down, we become more aware. Sometimes people eat out of habit, but when we become more mindful, we start to notice patterns that, once understood, can help us harness a whole new way of eating and living."

Being mindful when eating is a powerful mindfulness tool to help us make better choices. And our choices can give us a profound mind-body experience. It taps into every aspect of our health. Bringing calm and focus to our eating can shift our mindset and benefit our physical, mental, and spiritual state in the following ways:

1. **Finding more joy in eating:** Calm and focused eating encourages mindfulness, allowing you to savor each bite, appreciate flavors, and make more conscious food choices.

2. **Weight management:** Being present while eating can help you recognize when you're full, reducing the likelihood of overeating and supporting weight management.

3. **Reduced stress:** Maintaining a serene state of mind while eating has the potential to reduce stress, thereby suppressing the release of cortisol and averting a surge in glucose levels. This, in turn, promotes improved digestion and enhances nutrient absorption.

4. **Improved digestion:** Focusing on your food promotes proper chewing and digestion, reducing digestive discomfort and enhancing nutrient utilization.

5. **Better food choices:** Mindful eating helps you make healthier food choices as you become more attuned to your body's needs and cravings.

6. **Emotional eating awareness:** Practicing mindfulness over time allows you to differentiate between physical hunger and emotional cravings, reducing impulsive eating.

7. **Blood sugar control:** Eating mindfully may help regulate blood sugar levels, which is beneficial for individuals with diabetes or those at risk.

8. **Gratitude mindset:** Taking time to enjoy your meals fosters a deeper appreciation for food and its role in nourishing your body.

9. **Positive relationships:** Developing a calm and focused approach to eating can help you cultivate not only a better relationship with food but also with others.

Self-Healing Invitation: Mindfulness Eating

Incorporating a mindfulness eating practice into your daily life is quite simple and can be practiced in, again, as little as 10 minutes. Here are a few short practices you can try:

Mindful Breathing:

1. Find a quiet place to sit comfortably.
2. Take a few deep breaths to center yourself.
3. As you start eating, focus on your breath. Inhale and exhale with mindfulness awareness.
4. Bring your attention to the present moment, allowing thoughts about your day to fade away.

Sensory Eating:

1. Take a moment to look at your food. Observe its colors, textures, and shapes.
2. Close your eyes and take a deep breath. Inhale the aroma of the food.
3. As you take your first bite, pay attention to the taste and texture. Chew slowly and savor each moment.
4. Notice any sounds associated with eating.

Gratitude:

1. Before you start eating, take a moment to express gratitude for your food.
2. As you eat, reflect on the journey of the food from its source to your plate.
3. With each bite, think about the people involved in growing, harvesting, and preparing the food.
4. Thank all those involved in bringing this food to you at this moment.

Conscious Awareness Eating:

1. Take a small bite of your food and put your utensils down.
2. Chew slowly and deliberately, paying attention to the taste and texture.
3. Try to identify each flavor and how it evolves as you continue chewing.
4. Only pick up your utensils for the next bite once you've fully swallowed the previous one.

Mindful Reflection:

1. Before you start eating, take a moment to set an intention for your meal. It could be to eat with gratitude, to savor each bite, or to eat with awareness.
2. Periodically check in with yourself throughout the meal. Are you still aligned with your intention? If not, gently guide your focus back to the present moment.

Download and print your Self-Healing Invitation here:

The key to mindful eating is to be fully present and engaged with the experience of eating. These practices can help cultivate a greater awareness of your relationship with food and promote a sense of well-being.

What areas of your life can mindfulness eating help to support?

Once I was able to start repairing my relationship with food, everything else about my life started to improve. My friendships were stronger. I felt more like my true self, like I didn't have to lie about who I was. I felt happy and alive, and I accepted myself more readily. I started dating a guy with whom I fell madly in love, and we stayed together for seven wonderful years. I pursued a Master's degree in writing and publishing and built a career in corporate marketing for the next fifteen years. I experienced less chaos and more balance, and I finally felt put back together again, like my life had a purpose.

A worksheet on the next page will help you track your progress as you practice mindfulness movement and eating. Notice how what you eat and how you move affect your mood from day to day and modify it as you need. Drink plenty of water, get plenty of rest, and implement your self-care.

Trackers are a great way to notice patterns that work or don't work for you. For example, you may notice that on the days when you do intense exercise, you may sleep better or worse. You may find that certain foods always affect your mood in the same way, or that you're not drinking enough water or implementing enough restorative time. Try it out for a few weeks and see what new awareness comes to you. If we don't track, we don't know what has to change.

And if nothing changes, nothing changes!

DATE: [_____]

M T W T F S S

wellness
tracker

DAILY GOALS:

_____

_____

NUTRITION TRACKER

Water	Breakfast	Lunch	Dinner	Snacks	Sweets & Desserts
◊◊◊ ◊◊◊ ◊◊◊ ◊◊◊					

WORKOUT PLAN   EXERCISE LOG

#	Exercise type	Sets	Reps	Intensity	X/✓	Sets	Reps	Intensity
1.								
2.								
3.								
4.								
5.								
6.								
7.								
8.								
9.								
10.								
11.								
12.								
13.								
14.								
15.								

MOOD AND ENERGY LEVELS   REST AND RECOVERY

Time	Type

CONNECTION

Chapter 9: Connection Is Power

"Shame corrodes the very part of us that believes we are capable of change." — Brené Brown

When I was in my late 30s and living with my mom, I went out of my way to avoid everyone. I completely disconnected and hid in my bedroom with my cat. My drinking was out of control. I went to jail twice, lost my driver's license, got fired from jobs, ruined my career, broke up with my boyfriend, and severed ties with my dad. I was financially broke, spiritually bankrupt, and emotionally disconnected.

My family was so disgusted with who I had become. My brother would later tell me that trying to talk to me was like talking to a shell of a person; it was excruciating. There was nothing there; there was no emotion, reaction, movement, or response. I was so ashamed of who I was, and I was so consumed with guilt that I cut myself off from everyone if they hadn't cut me off first. Of course, I acted as if I didn't care about anyone or anything because I was afraid to admit how I really felt inside. Opening myself up to that conversation would mean I'd have to confront my problem with alcohol, and I wasn't willing to do that.

I chose not to share in the joy and excitement of my high school and college friends reaching milestones in their lives, such as getting married, having their first baby, or getting big promotions. When class reunions came around, I didn't even reply to the invitation. Why would I show up? I had absolutely nothing to show for my life. I was full of self-pity, and while they were thriving and growing, building careers and having families, I was sitting on my bed at my mom's house, drinking from a vodka bottle and watching soap operas. How would that fly at a college reunion? I felt like a complete failure, and I didn't want to have to explain myself or make up a story that would paint a false picture of my life. I just wanted to avoid it altogether. Isolating was much easier.

After my second DUI arrest when I was thirty-two years old, the court ordered me to go to twelve recovery meetings and to bring along a paper for the chairperson to sign so that my probation officer could be sure that I went. I was horrified at the thought of walking into my first meeting, not knowing what to expect or who I would see there. I imagined only what I'd seen on TV or heard people describe alcoholics to look like—dirty and unkept, pushing around shopping carts, collecting garbage. To my surprise, this wasn't what I found at all.

At my first meeting, I looked around and saw women in business suits and others in golf attire, any of whom could've been one of my mom's friends. The women were of every age, race, and body type. They wore anything from ripped jeans and graphic tees to sun dresses or yoga pants. There was short hair, dyed hair, silver hair, and no hair. They were all talking with each other, hugging, smiling, and laughing. There was no division of class here. Everyone seemed to be friends.

I remember a young girl walking into the meeting with her baby. She was very pretty and well put together. She looked to be around my age. She was a new mom, full of gratitude for her blessing. The other ladies gathered around, taking turns holding her child. She looked so happy. I sat there studying her. I just couldn't have pictured her as a drunk, and I found myself curious as to what happened in the lives of these women that led them here, to the rooms of recovery.

Still, I wouldn't engage. I sat in a corner and didn't make eye contact with anyone because once I did, I knew that person would come find me to talk to me after the meeting. I felt like prey as a newcomer, new blood. It was like being surrounded by vampires looking for their next meal. I understood their mission was to help people get sober, but I was only there to satisfy the courts.

After the meeting, I'd quickly get my paper signed and leave. I wasn't ready for the help yet because that would mean admitting I was one of them, an alcoholic, and I didn't think I was. Yet I was full of guilt and shame for the way I was living my life.

After I completed my twelve meetings, I felt like it might be a good idea to keep going. I actually enjoyed listening to other people's stories, even if I didn't want to share my own. I could resonate with a lot of them, which I think scared me and calmed me down at the same time. It was like I felt like I belonged there, but I didn't want to belong. I wanted to be normal. So, I'd drink instead and avoid going, which made me feel even more ashamed. Why show up to a support group when I really don't want the support? I still wasn't willing to give long-term sobriety a chance, and it would piss me off when someone tried to convince me to do so. I didn't like anyone telling me what to do when it came to my drinking.

Brené Brown says, "Courage over comfort. You have to walk through vulnerability to get courage. Therefore...embrace the suck." I wasn't yet open to being vulnerable. That was too risky. What would people say? The reaction I got at home to the damage I was inflicting on myself was enough to shut me down. I assumed anyone I opened up to would react the same way. I was embarrassed of myself, yet keeping it all inside was slowly killing me. I hadn't yet learned that vulnerability was the key to cracking myself open to healing. Without the crack, the healing could not begin.

Out of Isolation

I was thirty-nine when I got sober in 2011, seven long years after my second arrest and two years after my third. The response from those who didn't have an alcohol problem was always, *"Haven't you had enough? What's it going to take?"* I had no response because I didn't know what it would take. I couldn't understand it myself. All I knew about alcoholism was what I learned in DUI school about it being a trifold disease, a physical allergy, a mental obsession, and a spiritual malady. I denied having any of the three.

On May 25, 2011, the day I had my last drink before riding my bike over to my friend's house, I didn't wake up and decide, "*Today is the day I have my last drink forever! Let me go ask for help.*" I was on the brink of something very bad happening. There are three things they say will happen to an alcoholic who doesn't stop drinking. Jail, institutions, and death, and I had already experienced two of them. I truly believe it was divine intervention that saved me from experiencing the third. I don't know why my life was spared so many times, only that there was a greater purpose for my life. I didn't realize that then, but I do now.

I always thought my mom and my brothers would be there to catch me when I fell. They had proven that to me over and over again. But on this day, the day I had my last drink, I went to detox and never returned home. After five days there, my mom told me I was on my own, to which I went to my brother's house before ending up at the homeless shelter.

I remember feeling tossed out, like an old, dirty rag.

If my brother had let me crash at his place indefinitely, I can only imagine how much further down this highway to hell I would have gone. His "abandoning me" was the ultimate act of compassion. He knew I could get sober more than I believed I could.

I disconnected from my family just long enough to get my head on straight. I kept myself from trying to call them so I could prove to myself that I was doing this for me and not for anyone else. Despite the damage I had done and the pain I had inflicted on them, I knew I had to disconnect before connecting again. So, I stayed close to the fellowship in my recovery program. I once again found myself in meetings, but this time, I was willing to open up. The worst was over with, and the only way was forward.

Raising my hand and saying, "Hi, I'm Christina, and I'm an alcoholic," for the first time, and meaning it, was the most courageous thing I had ever done. It was alarmingly easy to say out loud, and after the first time I admitted it to everyone in the room, I felt a huge weight lift off of me. This was a feeling I had waited to feel for a long time—relief from the admission, from being honest about who I really was. I didn't have to lie or hide anymore. I was safe and with a community of people just like me.

I underestimated the power of connection when I was drinking, and I certainly didn't pay attention to it while sitting in meetings and denying my disease. Over the years, I have watched so many people heal from their alcoholic wounds and thrive in their lives with the support of community in recovery programs. People need people, and in this particular space, where others like me came in feeling isolated, defeated, and hopeless, it was each other who gave us the hope to carry on. It was the community that gave us the strength to get through one more day without a drink. It was the magic of fellowship, where men and women aligned in their mission to help others like themselves, that gave us the courage to make ourselves vulnerable and share our stories. As a result, this coming together fueled our passion for living sober and serving others.

Community is often where we can find the safety and security to open ourselves up and release the demons that want to hold us down. It is too much to handle alone, and so the power of community is something I see as divine. Community is God working through many people all at once, and it is one of the strongest forces of energy I have ever experienced.

When I was a year sober, I started running recovery meetings in the county jail as part of my service work. It was something I felt called to do in early sobriety because I remember attending meetings when I'd been incarcerated for my drinking. Some of these women were behind bars for a long time and needed something to give them hope. Part of my redemption was to pay it forward and share my experience, strength, and hope with them.

I offered this service for five years and witnessed the same women coming in and out of jail like a revolving door. Orange jumpsuits meant felonies and green meant misdemeanors. Some of the inmates wore orange like a badge of honor. I remember the first time I went to jail; I was accidentally given an orange jumpsuit. I'd thought about turning it in for a green one but decided to keep my mouth shut, thinking maybe orange would keep people from messing with me. It seemed to do the trick.

When I first started this service work, meetings were held in the pods, which were communal areas where inmates congregated during the day. Everything was made of cold steel, from the bunks to the tables and chairs, right down to the toilets. Bathrooms had no doors, so everyone was in plain sight of the guards at all times, even during a shower. There were tiny windows where the wall met the ceiling, so you couldn't actually look outside. To me, that felt like torture, having a window but not being able to enjoy the view. The only thing you could see was a sliver of sky, showing you if it was sunny or cloudy, day or night.

The meetings were eventually moved to a classroom environment where I would sit in the front of the room like a teacher. At first, the inmates were quiet, showing no interest in engaging with me, just like a bunch of school kids on their first day of school. As I continued to show up for them, month after month, telling them about the time I spent in jail and found myself homeless, they slowly loosened up. They raised their hands, asked questions, and became eager to share more and more. Eventually, they started approaching me after the meetings to thank me and to talk more. They didn't hold back their tears after hearing about my journey back to health and happiness, telling me how they felt hopeful and less scared for the first time. They realized we had something in common, and although the details of my story were different from theirs, we shared the same pain.

One young woman came up to me after a meeting and thanked me for telling her about the homeless shelter where I lived for the first four months of my sobriety because she was going to that same shelter after she was released from jail. I'll never forget her telling me, "I was terrified, even more so than being here in jail, but I'm not scared anymore, thanks to you." If hugs had been allowed, there most definitely would have been many after those meetings.

There was another woman who seemed like she was trying to intimidate me. She would come to every meeting, possibly just to get out of the pod, and sit slumped in her chair, legs spread wide in her oversized orange jumpsuit, arms crossed tightly across her chest. As I spoke, she'd glare at me. She had *you're a joke* written all over her face, and I was convinced she'd never warm up to the conversation. To my surprise, after a few months, I noticed her sitting more upright in her chair, more attentive to the discussion, and seemingly interested in what I had to say. She came up to me after a meeting one night, shook my hand, and said, "Thank you. I could really relate to a lot of what you said." I talked more with her and had the opportunity to learn more of her story. She was off to prison, but she said she would seek meetings there.

In the most unlikely of places, connection has the power to change your life. It will give you the courage to make yourself vulnerable, and when it feels aligned, it will teach you how to trust. Learning to trust others fosters a sense of safety and support, which enhances our resilience, giving us a sense of emotional well-being. When I made myself vulnerable to sharing my stories in the jail, I made this group of women trust in me enough to feel comfortable opening up. Together, we created a foundation for open communication, mutual understanding, and collaboration.

I would always tell the women at the end of each meeting, "You all are helping me as much, if not more than I am helping you right now." Every time I walked out, I felt empowered, knowing I was making a difference.

Being of service to others and creating a community can benefit us in numerous ways. They can help to:

1. **Enhance well-being:** Helping others can boost our mood and sense of well-being. Acts of kindness and service release endorphins, often referred to as the "helper's high."
2. **Build connections:** Service fosters a sense of community and connection. It helps build meaningful relationships and strengthens social bonds.
3. **Increase empathy and compassion:** By serving others, we develop a deeper understanding of different perspectives and experiences, strengthening our empathy and compassion for others.
4. **Boost self-esteem:** Knowing we have made a positive impact on someone else's life can enhance our self-worth and confidence.
5. **Provide purpose:** Engaging in acts of service can give us a sense of purpose and direction, contributing to a more fulfilling life.
6. **Reduce stress and anxiety:** Helping others can shift our focus away from our own worries, reducing stress and anxiety.
7. **Encourage gratitude:** Serving others often makes us more aware of our own blessings, fostering a sense of gratitude.
8. **Promote personal growth:** Service can challenge us to step out of our comfort zones, promoting personal growth and development.

I ran into some of these women later on at recovery meetings after they were released from jail. The meetings in jail gave them a chance to consider their choices about the future. Jail is a place where isolation can take you down a dark path because it's just as easy to be isolated in your mind as it is to be physically isolated. When I was isolated in my room, I at least had a mom who tried to encourage me to get better. Jail isn't necessarily a place where one is surrounded by a support system. I had the amazing privilege of supporting them and helping them foster their own community inside the jail, where they could continue their sober work, share their experiences with each other, and pray together. I left them with a message of what life could look like if they chose the path I did. They realized they had the opportunity to better their own lives and be of service to others, contributing to the ripple effect of inner peace and happiness in the world.

Connecting with these women was easy, not just because we had something in common, but because I could show up as my authentic self without judgment or expectation. I was no better than or less than the women in that room. We shared the common bond of addiction, and my job was to create a safe space where we could talk about our experiences freely and confidentially.

If we want to thrive, we need to show up for ourselves and others in the community.

We may have been taught that opening ourselves up to others isn't the answer or that, in hard times, things are better kept to ourselves. We may have been made to believe that vulnerability makes us look weak. Maybe we experienced being shut down by others when we tried to communicate. Any of these could make us feel unsafe to reveal our truths to someone, so we build up walls for security.

The reality, though, is that vulnerability is the antidote for shame. As I said earlier, once we can crack ourselves open, just a tiny bit, we allow the light to enter our hearts, and healing becomes possible.

Whatever the reason for this need to isolate, seeking comfort in aloneness is not always the healthy option. Prolonged isolation can lead to:

- Heightened stress levels
- Cognitive decline
- Sleep problems
- Weakened immune system
- Cardiovascular issues
- Weight fluctuations

- Decreased physical activity
- Overall lower quality of life

As I mentioned, isolating doesn't require that you are physically alone. You can be sitting in a crowded room and still feel alone there. I remember sitting in meetings before I was sober, surrounded by people just like myself, and still feeling alone. I had the opportunity to connect but was too afraid to speak up. So, I suffered in silence for a long time, unable to break from the shame.

Vulnerability can look different for everyone, but the one thing it requires is the courage to put ourselves out there despite the pain. It could be something as simple as introducing yourself to someone you've been wanting to meet at a party or asking your latest crush on a date, knowing you could be rejected or turned down. You could decide to finally apply for that job you've been wanting or, like me, quit your full-time job to write a book and start a business. Yikes! Maybe it's starting therapy or joining a trauma support group, where the only way to heal is to open up and let everyone see your wounds. In any case, in the face of uncertainty and at the risk of feeling emotionally hurt, we make ourselves vulnerable anyway because we see our potential for growth outside the walls we've been hiding behind.

Being a part of a community and opening ourselves up reinforces a variety of healthy behaviors that benefit all involved. This includes:

- **Stress reduction:** Engaging with others can help lower stress levels and improve overall emotional resilience.
- **Physical health:** Community involvement often includes physical activities and group exercises, contributing to better physical health and overall fitness.
- **Sense of belonging:** Being part of a community fosters a sense of belonging and connectedness, which positively impacts self-esteem and happiness.

- **Knowledge sharing:** Communities offer a platform for exchanging information, ideas, and experiences, empowering individuals to make more informed decisions and giving them a boost of confidence and self-trust.
- **Accountability:** In a community setting, individuals may feel accountable for their goals, leading to increased motivation and adherence to healthy habits.
- **Sense of purpose:** Active participation in a community can give individuals a sense of purpose and fulfillment, promoting a more positive outlook on life.
- **Longevity:** The "Harvard Study of Adult Development," one of the longest-running studies on adult life, suggests that individuals with strong social connections and community involvement tend to live longer and enjoy better overall health outcomes.

Sobriety gave me the opportunity to come alive again. After years of not knowing how to make genuine connections with people and sustain those relationships, I finally learned how. Although I had friends over the years, I didn't nurture them into my adulthood. I always thought friendships came and went. High school friends were my friends between the ages of fourteen and eighteen, and college friends were my friends until I was twenty-two. There were a few friendships that survived my twenties, but it wasn't until I was in my forties and sober that I was able to make meaningful friendships and recognize the value they brought to my life.

Looking back, I never did run with a specific tribe of friends. I was more of a floater, sitting at different lunch tables each school year, having a new best friend every few months, and hanging out with whoever was actively involved in my extra-curricular activities. Friends were seasonal. My tennis friends were there in the fall, theater friends in the winter, and summer friends at the Jersey Shore. It was like they had their own place, time, and purpose in my life. I valued them in the moment but then easily let them slip away.

When I was a drinker, the only criterion you needed to be my friend was to be a drinker. Those were the friends I kept for a long time, to fill my weekends or to have someone to accompany me to bars to meet guys. Once I got sober, I am happy to say that I reconnected with a few women whom I drank with back in the day and was able to nurture a healthier version of friendship. So, not all friendships died with my drinking.

Learning how to interact with other women in recovery created a foundation from which I could build and nurture relationships. It started in a small space with women just like me, giving me the confidence to be vulnerable and trust others. Over time, with intention and practice, I formed new friendships and created a sense of community with like-minded people.

Last year, for my fifty-second birthday, at thirteen years sober, I invited eight women to dinner at a Japanese steak house. I thought it would be fun for all of us to sit around the hibachi grill, get to know one another, and eat some really good food. I had a personal friendship with each of these women, but none of them had a friendship with each other.

Although we weren't a "circle of friends" that ran together, we were all connected that night, telling stories and laughing. I remember looking around the table, observing strangers becoming friends, and thought, *thirteen years ago, I didn't have two people to call to celebrate my birthday with me.* Since that night, we've formed a text group called "The Girls." We get together periodically for dinner or to go to events in town. I noticed them becoming friends on Facebook, getting together on their own, supporting each other's businesses, and empowering each other online.

Finding community gave me the support, understanding, and accountability I needed to not only develop relationships but learn to love myself again. I moved from a place of selfishness and ego to awareness and acceptance of others. The world didn't revolve around me and my pain, and when I was given the opportunity to be of service, I found compassion, empathy, and love.

Self-Healing Invitation: Connection

The following exercise can help you understand the vital role that connection can or has played in your personal healing and growth.

Instructions: Find a quiet, comfortable space where you can focus without interruptions. Take a few deep breaths to center yourself before you begin.

Step 1: Reflect on your relationships

- Think about the people in your life who have supported you through a healing journey. This could include family, friends, mentors, or support groups.
- Write down the names of these individuals and the specific ways they have contributed to your growth and healing.

Step 2: Assess the impact of connection

- Reflect on how these connections have influenced your journey. Consider both the emotional and practical support you have received.
- Ask yourself the following questions and jot down your thoughts:
    - How have these relationships helped you overcome challenges?
    - What lessons have you learned from these connections?
- How has the power of connection contributed to your sense of self-worth and empowerment?

Step 3: Express gratitude

- Take a moment to express gratitude for the connections you have. Write a short note or letter to one or more of the individuals who have made a significant impact on your life. This can be a private reflection or something you choose to share with them.

Step 4: Identify future opportunities for connection

- Think about ways you can continue to foster meaningful connections in your life. Identify at least two actions you can take to strengthen your existing relationships or build new ones.
- Write down these actions and make a commitment to follow through with them.

Step 5: Reflect on your own role

- Consider how you can be a source of connection and support for others. Reflect on the ways you can give back and help others in their journeys.
- Write down a few ideas on how you can offer support, encouragement, or mentorship to those who may need it. Take a few moments to sit with your reflections. Acknowledge the power of connection in your life and the reciprocal nature of giving and receiving support. Remember that fostering meaningful connections is a continuous process that enriches both your life and the lives of others.

Download and print your Self-Healing Invitation here:

Now that we've explored the significance of connecting with others, it's time to turn our focus inward and delve into the vital journey of reconnecting with ourselves.

Chapter 10: Reconnecting With Self

I spent the first few years of my recovery from alcoholism rebuilding my life with foundational things like a home, a job, health insurance, a bank account, and a driver's license. I made some friends at my new job and slowly started to feel like my life was normal again. For years, it had been one crisis or hardship after another, and the more I drank, the worse I made it. As a sober woman, I finally felt like I was a part of something bigger than myself instead of being alone. I was learning how to connect more meaningfully with others and to love myself again as I worked through my recovery program.

I stayed away from dating so I could focus on my well-being. I admit that part of me didn't want to date because I was still ashamed of my past and the fact that I'd been driving around with a breathalyzer in my car for two years. My bully voice would taunt me all the time and tell me that no decent guy would want to date a girl who had been to jail and spent her Saturday nights in recovery meetings. So, during that time, I channeled all my energy into rebuilding my life and getting to know myself again.

My friends finally convinced me to use some of the online dating sites. As apprehensive as I was, I set up a profile and started practicing having conversations with men. In fact, I even scored a few dates and found the practice of dating both fun and empowering.

I started chatting with a guy named Ben. He was awfully good looking and had that "bad boy" look that I was always drawn to. He wasn't from my area, but was still close enough where we could meet and see what came of it. "Don't limit yourself," my friends would say.

We met up at a coffee shop near me. I used this coffee shop for all of my first dates. It always felt safe enough, and since I didn't drink, I didn't have to worry about explaining why I wasn't drinking.

The conversation with Ben was refreshingly easy. He seemed humble and easygoing. There was no agenda, just talk, and we chatted for a good few hours. I felt at ease with Ben. There were no red flags. I decided I would go out with him again.

Ben and I became close friends at first. We enjoyed movies and coffee, and he even helped with things around my condo. He didn't really drink, so the fact that I was sober was never an issue. He was kind to other people—holding doors for women, assisting the elderly, and giving generously without expecting anything in return. I found myself confiding in him like I would a girlfriend, and it wasn't long before we became best friends.

I was developing feelings for him and he for me. The connection was undeniable. At first it scared me. But my feelings for him were too strong for me to ignore. I just wanted it to be the absolute right choice. I had made so many bad choices in the past. Then, on my birthday, we shared our first kiss. It was one of those kisses that made my knees weak. In that moment I surrendered to my feelings and we declared ourselves a couple.

I was continually amazed that this love was real. He was easy to talk to and comfortable to be around. We laughed at silly things, shared secrets we'd never told anyone, and could finish each other's sentences. I'd tell my mother, "He's the best boyfriend I've ever had." He supported all my aspirations and understood my relentless drive to succeed. He never got upset about my demanding work schedule, which often consumed my holidays and weekends.

Six months into our courtship, I could tell that something was really off, but I didn't know what or why. The tension between us got pretty bad, and by the end of the summer, it exploded into an awful mess. It was heart-wrenching. I never thought this man would just stop loving me.

He was suddenly too busy to spend time with me, and when he did, his mood was quite different; it felt like he would rather be somewhere else. Even his tone with me was different. I couldn't understand why he seemed so disgusted with me. I didn't know how to respond or handle it. Our communication was broken, and if I tried to talk about our relationship, I felt like I was quickly shut down. He had his way of dealing with things, and I had mine. I wanted him to handle things my way. As much as I pointed fingers at him, I wasn't accepting him for who he was. I started feeling like the desperate one, clinging to a relationship that was over but trying to force it back together. It only made things worse.

The fighting got ugly, and I became fragile to it. I started walking on eggshells, afraid to say anything. The confrontation made me so uncomfortable, but he seemed to thrive in it. He would always win any verbal showdown we had. I loved him so much. I just wanted him to love me back again like he did in the beginning.

After our final fight, I was so disgusted and resentful. I swore I would never talk to him again. The truth was, I didn't want it to be over. I wanted it to be like it was in the beginning. Where did it all go wrong? I thought maybe after he had some time to cool off, he'd reach out and want to reconcile. But that didn't happen immediately.

I started to unravel. I stopped going to my recovery meetings. All of my attention was on the relationship and trying to figure out what went wrong. We eventually started talking again, and I thought we'd get back together, but we just weren't on the same page. His actions were confusing, and I could never tell what he wanted. It was like he enjoyed my attention but wanted to keep his options open. This made me feel even more desperate. I'd watch him on social media and try to figure out what he was up to and who he was talking to. I became obsessed.

Our relationship felt like a roller coaster ride. We were on again and off again and I never knew where we stood with each other. It felt like a game that I just couldn't win. How far down would I go to get his attention or win his love back? At times, it seemed like he wanted us to get back together, so I would think we were moving forward, and then he'd get quiet or disappear for a while. Then I'd see him back on dating sites, which was completely his right, and I figured we were done. After a while, I didn't even bother trying to have a conversation about it. It felt humiliating.

This back-and-forth made me feel crazy, and the longer it continued, the deeper I got. My friends got tired of hearing about it and couldn't understand why I let this continue. It's not that I didn't value their advice. It was that I couldn't let go. I couldn't accept that someone didn't want me. I couldn't take feeling rejected and abandoned. The problem wasn't him; it was me, but I could not see it at the time. I spent so much of my energy trying to figure him out, and the truth was, it really wasn't my business who he was.

Through our entanglement, I became a totally different person. The strength, resilience, and strong sense of self I found in my recovery were all gone, as if a tidal wave came in and washed them all away. It was traumatic emotionally and sent me into a downward spiral of alcoholic tendencies like obsessiveness, compulsiveness, manipulation, and disillusionment. Although I didn't drink, my alcoholic behaviors were fired up again, and I felt stuck. I probably have ten journals filled with nothing but stories about him, with pages tagged and highlighted as I tried to understand Ben, the enigma.

It was an addiction. He was my alcohol. Maybe at first, there was an infatuation that felt like love, but my behavior over the course of this relationship was not real love, and it definitely was not me loving myself.

This new low was a pivotal moment in my recovery, and I had to once again, surrender and let go of something I felt attached to. Early in sobriety, the excitement of reconnecting with others after a long period of isolation can make us vulnerable to inviting people into our lives before we are ready for them. At that time, I hadn't yet learned how to set and maintain boundaries and didn't fully understand what I needed to emotionally protect myself.

My therapist recommended a book called *Codependent No More* by Melody Beattie, which put me on a trajectory toward reconnecting with myself again. Beattie defines a codependent person as "one who has let another person's behavior affect him or her and who is obsessed with controlling that person's behavior." I was like, *holy crap, that's me!*

I'd had enough. Recognizing myself in the book made me realize I needed to start detaching from this man or risk being stuck in a cycle with him for years. It didn't happen immediately. It took a while to completely free myself and emotionally detach. I had loved him so deeply. We had a connection that felt like electricity. I valued our love so much that letting him go was as hard as letting my alcohol go.

There was no dramatic break, as we weren't in a committed relationship; instead, I worked on detaching gradually and quietly. I didn't cut off contact or have a formal conversation with him about it. That never worked. I simply made a decision and committed to myself, then began to step back. I recognized and took advantage of those periods of silence between us, using the time to strengthen my relationship with myself instead of focusing on him. It was like doing pushups when he wasn't around, getting stronger and stronger each time. Eventually, I became more invested in myself than in him.

I stopped going to my therapist because while talk therapy helps many people for many different reasons, it made me sick of hearing myself talk about him. I started looking for different options for support aside from my recovery program. I'd listen to life coaches online talking about breakups, entanglements, reconciliations, and manifesting. I was inspired by people like Shelly Bullard talking about how she manifested love into her life and how I could do it too. Helena Hart offered compassion to those just after a breakup and taught them how to pull their lives back together. Abraham Hicks was my go-to guru for all things Law of Attraction which I became completely obsessed with.

Self-Healing Invitation: Reclaim Your Power

I'll never forget this one video on YouTube by Helena Hart on taking back your power after a breakup. I remember standing in my kitchen listening to her as she walked us through a five-step process on how to remove your energy from an ex-boyfriend and put it back on yourself. I now use my own version of this in a three-step process with my own clients. You can apply this to anything you are obsessing about, person, place or thing.

Step 1: Visualize peeling your energy off your object of obsession: Sit quietly, close your eyes, and visualize peeling something off their body. Maybe it's a sticker or a banana peel. When I first did this exercise, I pictured a leech as if I was the leech clinging to him. Whatever you see, peel it off.

Step 2: Put that energy back on yourself. Now place that thing you peeled off of your object of obsession and stick it over your heart. As you do, imagine it turning into a vibrant ball of light, giving you nourishing energy. Picture it lighting up every part of you, rejuvenating and empowering you. As you breathe into this new energy, notice how your emotions shift. You're no longer the leech but a source of powerful feminine energy, feeling renewed, empowered, and a bit like a badass.

Step 3: Choose one thing you enjoy and focus on that. Visualize yourself living your best life and engaging in activities that bring you joy. Take yourself on a vision quest, imagining the life you desire. Afterward, start creating that life by taking one action, big or small, that brings you closer to that dream. Create a vision board and concentrate on one aspect at a time. Let it represent all you want, like a thriving career, a happy relationship, a beautiful home, a vacation in Greece, or a thriving community of friends.

Download and print your Self-Healing Invitation here:

Each time I used my mind to envision where I wanted to be, I felt a surge of excitement. I became more attuned to what ignited my passion and gained clarity on my vision. I felt like I wanted to help others break free too and reclaim their power—not just from relationships, but from all sorts of addictions that hold us back.

With a renewed interest in myself, I explored ways that I could help other women like me. I started joining wellness communities, shared my passion for essential oil therapies, and became certified as an integrative nutrition health coach. While I wasn't sure where this new path would lead, I remained committed to my dream and thoroughly enjoyed every step of the journey.

For a long time, I felt sorry for myself, focusing on how I was wronged and waiting for Ben to acknowledge his behaviors instead of examining the toxicity I contributed to the relationship. I failed to recognize the power I had to thrive and instead gave all my power to him. I finally learned to let go of my need for an explanation, an apology, or for him to understand or admit his part. Recovery had taught me that I was only responsible for keeping my side of the street clean. I am not responsible for the thoughts, words, or actions of another, and so I released myself from the grip I had on him, and I was free.

My time in my health coaching program was a transformative experience that served as a healing journey and provided me with the much-needed guidance I was seeking. By honing in on my desires and aspirations, I began to attract opportunities that resonated with my objectives. It felt akin to tracing a trail of breadcrumbs; the more breadcrumbs I discovered, the richer and more expansive my world became.

The reason I share this story is to show you how messy the mind can become and how, at the same time, it has the power to heal if we just take hold of the reins. I wasn't crazy. I was lost. I had disconnected from myself, but I got to know an even better version on the other side.

This was my time.

Self-Healing Invitation: Open the Intuitive Mind

Here is a mindfulness practice I love that I learned from one of my favorite psychic healers. I've used this practice to help me unlock my subconscious and open my intuitive mind, my place of wisdom. This exercise helps us to reveal things about ourselves that can be helpful in healing trauma, responding to challenging life moments, squashing resentments, and showing more compassion towards others and ourselves.

Write a letter and address it to your highest self. You can start with "Dear Beloved" or "Dear Highest Self." Whatever calls to you.

To prepare, get your favorite journal, find a cozy spot where you can have some privacy, prepare a cup of tea or coffee, and just write down whatever comes up. This writing should be free-flowing, uninterrupted, and continuous. It doesn't matter if the thoughts are not connected or don't make sense. You may even find that you recall memories more easily or have moments of clarity about something you've been trying to figure out.

This can be a helpful tool for self-reflection and understanding the mind's processes. It can also help reveal to you the source of your pain or struggle. Uncovering these aspects of ourselves that we've repressed or ignored is a huge step forward in understanding who we are. This allows you to mend relationships or make new connections that are truly aligned with you.

Practice this daily for two weeks, and watch the answers come to you.

What did you uncover about yourself and the relationships in your life?

What desires have you discovered?

What lights you up with joy?

What is the vision of your future self?

Download and print your Self-Healing Invitation here:

Cultivating a deep connection with ourselves and others generates a harmonious synergy that enriches our emotional well-being and serves as a cornerstone for sustaining holistic health and profound joy. This intricate web of connections not only nurtures our inner and outer worlds but also prepares us to embrace the gifts of spiritual connection. The power of spiritual connection is immense and often overlooked, yet it plays an important role in any transformative journey, guiding us toward a deeper understanding of life and our place within it. Let's take a closer look at that now.

Chapter 11: Connecting With a Higher Power

In 2008, in an attempt to save my job and my relationship with my boyfriend at the time, I spent thirty days at an in-patient recovery center. It didn't look or feel like your typical rehabilitation center. It was located in a picturesque town nestled in the mountains and had a charming New England vibe. When I first arrived there, I told myself that perhaps I would never leave. This is the type of place I had always dreamed of escaping to.

Having always been a lover of the outdoors, this was heaven to me. The rooms felt more like being at a bed and breakfast, adorned with country charm from the furniture to the curtains, all the way down to the bedspreads. There was a central gathering place that resembled an old barn where we ate our meals, held our recovery meetings, and met up for evening activities like movies, speaking engagements, and games.

There was something magical about being there. It was mid-October, and the colors of the leaves were changing. The air was crisp, the sun still warm, and at night I would fall asleep to the sounds of crickets, cicadas, and owls coming from the woods outside my window. The feeling of being there brought me back to my childhood growing up in Tuxedo, New York.

The women who stayed in my house all became friends, even the ones who came in with resistance and wouldn't talk to anyone. After a few days, they even woke to the magic of this place and surrendered to being there. There was something about the pain we shared that brought us together in peace and harmony. I was making connections with other women for the first time in a long time, and it felt transformative. I remember all of us playing volleyball in the afternoon and how much we laughed together. I stopped for a moment, aware of how the laughter felt and the fact that I couldn't remember the last time I laughed at all, or even smiled, for that matter. At that moment, I felt like my life was going to change.

Although I did not stay sober after my visit there, I didn't consider it a waste of time. Nothing in life, not one experience we go through, is a waste of time. Everything has its place and purpose, and it's up to us to recognize, accept, and understand it.

The time I spent there played a significant role in my newfound relationship with God. I always believed in God but never felt a real connection to Him.

God is my Higher Power. Some may recognize their Higher Power as some other kind of source energy, like a tree, water, or an animal. For others, it's a feeling. What's great about choosing a Higher Power is that it's our choice and what feels right to us. The important thing is to believe in a power greater than ourselves that provides strength, guidance, and support during the recovery journey.

Perhaps it was the setting up in the mountains that made me feel closer to God, but it felt easy to talk to Him there. On some days, one of the staff members would take us on a hike, and I remember reaching the top of the mountain where we could see for miles and miles and thinking, *God is up here with me*. It was the most spiritual experience; one I had never experienced in a Church. Church and places of worship work beautifully for so many, but for me, I felt my Church outside, up here at the top of the mountain and on the trail surrounded by trees, animals, and small streams. I felt relieved that I had finally found Him. It wasn't that he was never there. It's just that I had been looking in the wrong place.

Maybe tapping into the spiritual aspect of yourself feels challenging. Or maybe it's an area of wellness you'd like to explore more deeply. Engaging in spirituality through practices like meditation, prayer, and mindfulness can reduce stress, improve mental and emotional well-being, and enhance overall health. Spirituality fosters positive emotions, supports healthy behaviors, and promotes resilience, leading to a greater sense of purpose and fulfillment in life. Additionally, being part of a supportive spiritual community can provide social connection and support, further benefiting health and well-being.

Since that visit to the recovery center, I have discovered many ways to connect to spiritual guidance. This guidance aligns me with my intuition, where the answers always are.

Ways to Connect Spiritually

Spirituality is a personal journey, so feel free to explore different practices and find what resonates most with you. It's okay to experiment and adapt your spiritual practice over time as you continue to grow and evolve on your journey. You'll notice that my list of ideas to get you started includes the same kinds of self-nurturing practices we've already explored throughout this book. By setting an intention before your practice, you can align yourself with the specific benefit the practice gives you.

1. **Meditation:** Practice mindfulness or guided meditation to cultivate present-moment awareness, reduce stress, and promote inner peace.
2. **Prayer:** Engage in prayer as a way to connect with a Higher Power, express gratitude, seek guidance, and find solace during challenging times. If you don't know where to start, just getting on your knees and asking for guidance is enough.
3. **Journaling:** Reflect on your thoughts, feelings, and experiences through journaling. This can help foster self-awareness, personal growth, and spiritual insight. Free writing first thing in the

morning is a great way to allow the subconscious mind to speak to us.

4. **Yoga:** Yoga can be a spiritual practice that integrates physical postures, breathwork, and meditation to promote holistic well-being and spiritual growth.

5. **Nature connection:** Spend time in nature to connect with the natural world, appreciate its beauty, and experience a sense of awe and wonder. Being in nature is a great way to feel grounded and receive wisdom from our intuitive minds.

6. **Gratitude practice:** Cultivate gratitude by regularly reflecting on and expressing appreciation for the blessings in your life, both big and small.

7. **Reading sacred texts:** Explore sacred texts from various spiritual traditions to gain wisdom, insight, and inspiration for your spiritual journey.

8. **Creative expression:** Express your spirituality through creative outlets such as art, music, dance, or writing, allowing your inner creativity to flow freely.

9. **Service and generosity:** Engage in acts of service and generosity to cultivate compassion, kindness, and a sense of connection with others.

10. **Silent retreats:** Attend a silent retreat or spend time in silent contemplation to deepen your spiritual practice and cultivate inner stillness and clarity.

11. **Sacred rituals:** Create your own sacred rituals or participate in traditional rituals from your cultural or spiritual background to honor significant life events or transitions.

12. **Community involvement:** Get involved in a spiritual community or group that aligns with your beliefs and values, providing opportunities for fellowship, support, and shared growth.

13. **Mindful movement:** Engage in mindful movement practices such as Tai Chi, qigong, or walking meditation to cultivate awareness of the body and breath.

Some of my favorite ways to tap into my spirituality are through energy healing practices like reiki or healing sound baths. While energy healing can be a powerful tool for spiritual connection and growth, it's also essential to integrate these practices with other aspects of spiritual exploration, such as meditation, prayer, or self-reflection, for a well-rounded approach to spirituality.

Energy healing modalities operate on the principle that we all possess a vital life force or energy, and imbalances in this energy can lead to physical, emotional, or spiritual disharmony. Engaging in energy healing practices can promote spiritual connection in several ways.

- **Awareness of energy**: Energy healing practices often involve becoming more attuned to the subtle energies within and around the body. This heightened awareness can lead to a deeper understanding of one's own energy system and its connection to the larger universe.
- **Balance and harmony**: Energy healing aims to restore balance and harmony to the body, mind, and spirit and promote the free flow of energy. This sense of equilibrium can foster a greater sense of spiritual well-being and connectedness.
- **Mind-body-spirit connection**: Energy healing approaches typically view the individual as a holistic being encompassing the mind, body, and spirit. By addressing energy imbalances at all levels, these practices facilitate integration and alignment, supporting spiritual growth and development.
- **Tapping into intuition**: Practitioners and recipients of energy healing often report experiencing intuitive insights, heightened awareness, or spiritual revelations during sessions which can deepen one's connection to their inner wisdom and spiritual guidance.

- **Self-healing and empowerment**: Engaging in energy healing practices empowers individuals to take an active role in their own healing and spiritual journey. By learning to work with their own energy systems, individuals can cultivate self-awareness, self-care, and self-empowerment.

Spiritual Guidance Through Grief

I'll never forget the day my cat crossed over the rainbow bridge. It was the first time I experienced the death of a being that was so close to me. It was emotionally excruciating, and I wasn't quite sure what to do with myself. She had been my family, and now I'd have to get used to coming home to a quiet house with no one there but me. Nothing would feel the same.

The next day, I went to work, and my store manager told me that she was leaving for another opportunity and offered me the job of running the store. She knew that I'd lost my cat the night before and was nervous to bring it up. My first reaction was a defensive one, and I said, "I can't do that! That wasn't in the plan!" My plan was to leave retail to start a health coaching business, not to step back into a store manager position where I would have to take on a world of responsibility again. She just said, "Christina, the company pays managers well. They really take care of their people. Just consider it."

She went into the back room onto a conference call, and I stood out on the sales floor all by myself. There were no customers. In the stillness, I thought about what she had said, and so I asked my cat up in heaven, "Linkin, what should I do?"

I immediately knew the answer to my own question. It was as if Linkin heard me and pointed me in the direction of my intuition. The more I thought about this opportunity, the more I realized how much I needed it. It was as if she was saying to me, "This is part of the journey. There's still more work for you to do here. You've got this."

Everything was all lined up for me. This opportunity came to me in divine timing. I lost one thing and gained another. My cat was no longer suffering, and I was no longer worrying. I could step into this new role and be all in. We were both free.

Grieving the loss of her was hard. I wasted no time and got into action right away, learning how to connect with Linkin in a different way. I allowed myself to feel the feelings, and I cried hard for the first two weeks when I came home at the end of each day. She used to sit in the front window and wait for me. I missed seeing her there when I pulled my car in, and I dreaded the drive home, knowing I would no longer see her there, looking for me. So, I refused to look up in the window anymore.

I sat on my bed and held onto her ashes. I read books and listened to animal communicators who taught me how to see her now that she was gone from the physical world. I opened myself up to receive the love and guidance from her from a different place and in a different way, and the grief eventually softened. I learned how to appreciate this new spiritual relationship with her and how to deal with death gracefully.

A few months later, Lucy came to me. Lucy looks just like Linkin but has a much more outgoing personality. I wasn't ready for a new cat, but she was ready for me, and I can't imagine my life without her. I can look up in the window again when I pull in at the end of the day and see her there. I see both of them there together because when I see Lucy, I know Linkin brought her to me.

Having a spiritual foundation with my Higher Power made it possible for me to believe I could continue a relationship with my beloved cat on the other side. Knowing that these spiritual energies existed brought me so much comfort while I was grieving. Understanding that I can have relationships with spiritual beings helped me through the grief when my father passed away, too.

The power of spiritual connections can help us find new purpose and meaning in our lives which can lead to positive actions in daily life. Some people who experience spiritual healing find positive body sensations and symptomatic relief from physical pain. Others find peace in having a greater sense of support, helping them to cope better with difficult decisions.

Self-Healing Invitation: Spiritual Connection

Let's try an exercise that can help you delve deeper into the nuances of your spiritual experience, uncovering layers of meaning and understanding that contribute to your personal and spiritual growth.

Describe a time in your life when you feel you've had a spiritual experience:

What thoughts or insights came to you during this experience?

How did your experience affect you afterward? Have there been any lasting changes in your beliefs, attitudes, or behaviors as a result?

How has this experience influenced your relationships or sense of community?

Download and print your Self-Healing Invitation here:

So far, we've explored how to harness the power of your mind and body to break free from old patterns, find healing, and reclaim a sense of control. Through mindfulness, self-compassion, nourishment, and connection, you've discovered tools that are already within your reach—tools to help you soften your inner critic, fuel your body with care, and align with your highest self.

Now, it's time to take these insights and transform them into the life you desire. In the following chapter, we'll put everything together, building a path toward creating the empowered, abundant life you're meant to live.

CREATE THE LIFE
YOU WANT

Chapter 12: Creating Time Abundance

I had a client, Suzanne, who had been living in chaos with a personal crisis for quite a few years before she reached out to me for help. She'd completed chemotherapy for breast cancer a year before and had been micro-managing her husband's drinking ever since. His drinking had been a problem for years. "I haven't even had a chance to heal myself since I stopped treatment," she said. She had spent so much time and energy taking care of him that she completely stopped taking care of herself—skipping her yoga classes after work, canceling plans with friends, or avoiding her favorite acupuncturist out of fear that her husband would be home by himself getting drunk. She felt like the only way to control his drinking was to be home watching his every move.

When he went to rehab for the fourth time, she knew she had an opportunity to start taking better care of herself. She'd reached her bottom and was exhausted, frustrated, resentful, and scattered, and desperately wanted to feel in control of her life again. She reached out to me to help her eliminate the overwhelm so she could start feeling better about herself and her life.

Suzanne didn't know exactly what she wanted to fix in her life when we started working together. The only thing she knew was that she didn't like how she was feeling, and something had to change. "I just feel all over the place," she told me. "I have all of these things I want to get back to doing, but I just don't know how to get there. Life still feels so chaotic."

On her assessment form, she indicated that she wanted to work on eating healthier and losing weight. She also mentioned wanting to get off some prescription medications and exercising more. These were things she felt like she needed to do, but she still wasn't sure what she wanted at the end of all of it except to feel peace again. This was the perfect place to start.

We don't have to have it all figured out to take the first step. Knowing whether we want to *feel* something or *not feel* something is enough in the beginning. Suzanne knew that something had to change, so we worked together to set her goals. I had her start with the holistic health wheel from Chapter 2, and from that exercise, she discovered that in order to feel less chaos and more balance, she needed to bring organization and structure back into her life. It was an eye-opener she didn't expect, but she was open to exploring a new way to manage her time.

Before we jumped into the time management piece, it was important to begin with Suzanne's mindset. We started with some of the mindfulness and mindset exercises from Chapters 3 and 4, specifically gratitude journaling and challenging her bully voice. Until we spent some time on these, she really hadn't noticed the stories she'd been telling herself. On one hand, she knew these stories weren't true. But on the other hand, she was still operating on false beliefs.

"I feel like if I say 'no' to people, I'll be disappointing them," she told me.

"What evidence do you have that tells you they would be disappointed?" I asked.

Sure enough, there was no evidence because it was a story she didn't even realize she was telling herself.

"I've spent so many years taking care of everyone else," she told me during another session. "I don't even know who I am anymore. I've lost my sense of self."

Right there, we could both clearly see that in order to reclaim her sense of self, she would have to learn how to set boundaries and put herself first. And to do that, she would have to change her belief that everyone would be disappointed if she made herself a priority. To change her belief, she would have to start telling herself a new story.

"I deserve to put myself first."

"I am worthy of putting myself first."

"No one is judging me for putting myself first."

"Making myself a priority is respecting myself, therefore teaching others to respect me."

Next, I walked her through a visualization practice where she envisioned a day in the life of her future self. I guided her with questions like:

How do you start your day?

What are you wearing?

How do you wear your hair?

What colors do you see?

Describe your house.

What sounds do you hear?

What do you do for work?

How are you feeling?

Where are you going?

Who are you with?

We got as detailed as we could during this "in the day of your future self" dream. I remember after we were done, she just said, "Wow," and sat in silence to take it all in. Seeing herself in that vision made her tear up and fueled her belief that she could have this life without all the stress. She could live how she wanted to live and be happy.

Initially, Suzanne felt overwhelmed and annoyed, believing everything was her husband's fault in their marriage. "If he would stop drinking, we wouldn't be here," she'd say. Although she would acknowledge her role, she still found herself blaming him for their current state of affairs, and if he only did what she wanted, she'd be happier. However, after working through the exercises and challenging the narratives she created, Suzanne was able to start shifting her perspective. She realized she was responsible for her own happiness and understood that doing things that made her feel good was within her power because she had the ability to choose.

Still feeling overwhelmed about how to fit everything in, I next walked Suzanne through a simple time management process that would help her identify how she was spending her time and teach her how to use time blocking to organize her days. Implementing a time management system helped pave the way for everything else to fall into place. If I'd started Suzanne with creating healthy habits and routines, it wouldn't have made sense to her, as she was feeling overwhelmed. The time management work came first, so the routines had a place to go.

During the process, she uncovered times in her day that she was underutilizing, like her mornings. We created a morning routine that included journaling, setting daily goals, declaring what energy she wanted to be in, setting intentions for inner peace and calm, and a gratitude list. This helped her to set the tone for her day, be in an abundance mindset, and feel more structured. Her morning routine also helped her with setting boundaries to protect her time. After some practice, she realized how much time and energy she had spent trying to control what was happening at home, somewhat like how I had tried to control and manipulate what happened with my ex-boyfriend. If she wasn't checking his phone, running home to "babysit," and micromanaging his every move, she was thinking about him, stewing with anger and resentment.

She was essentially breaking her own boundary, interrupting time for self-care to constantly check on him.

Suzanne had so many things she wanted to do when the time and space were given to her to do it, but she didn't know how to set it into motion. She had been living in chaos for so long with the frenetic energy of 'caretaking' for her husband that she didn't think there was anything she could do about it. She thought this was just the way it was. Needless to say, she was so relieved to learn that there was a solution for reclaiming her time and feeling less stressed.

After a while, the new time management system, which I will walk you through in this chapter, helped her to feel like she could breathe again. She woke up with a clear head because she had planned her week ahead of time with boundaries for her self-care. She started going back to yoga, where she could practice her meditation, breathing, and gentle movement; she returned to meal prepping for busy days at school as a teacher, so she could ensure she was nourishing herself; and she carved out time to go out with friends who fueled her with the positivity and joy she really needed.

She was grateful for the time management system because it set the foundation for her to build in healthy routines, adhere to her boundaries, and continue her healing journey post-cancer.

A Holistic Approach to Time

What I have found to be most interesting about time management is that it's not really about time at all. It's usually something that runs much deeper, making it challenging to manage time and live an abundant life. Even more, when life throws a curveball and knocks you off balance, like it did for Suzanne, it can feel like maintaining a sense of control is impossible. A time management system can be used as a tool for getting back on track and a way for you to uncover deeper aspects of yourself that affect how you live your life.

Let's look at this holistically and explore factors beyond scheduling that can help you understand your ability to manage time and feel in control.

Physical Factors

- **Low energy:** Lack of sleep, exercise, or nutritious food can result in low energy levels, impacting productivity. This can make your most important actions feel very overwhelming, causing you to procrastinate or panic, feeling like there isn't enough time.
- **Stress:** Stress causes fatigue, which makes it hard to stay focused and alert. Fatigue and brain fog interfere with efficient problem-solving and create a cycle where stress reduces productivity, which then increases stress further.
- **Brain health:** Poor nutrition, sleep, and exercise can also impact cognitive function, making it difficult to concentrate or make decisions.

Emotional Factors

- **Emotional overload:** Unresolved emotions such as anxiety, anger, or sadness can cause distraction or avoidance, complicating time management. Emotional overload can impair clear thinking and focused work, leading to frustration and feeling like giving up.
- **Fear of failure or success:** Fear of failure can cause us to procrastinate, which only prolongs our discomfort, while fear of success can cause us to fill our schedules with busy work rather than meaningful tasks that align with our goal. Some may avoid revenue-generating activities due to fear of managing large sums of money.
- **People pleasing:** The need to feel accepted by others causes us to say "yes" when we want to say "no," leaving little time for personal priorities. This can lead to burnout and feeling like we have no control over our time.

Spiritual Factors

- **Lack of purpose:** When we aren't clear on our life purpose, prioritizing tasks can feel impossible. Acting with no direction can make us feel defeated and out of alignment with our spiritual goals.
- **Disconnected with self:** Misalignment with our spiritual goals can make us lose our sense of self, causing us to drift through life without clear priorities and making it difficult to manage time effectively.
- **Inner peace and mindfulness**: A lack of mindfulness or spiritual grounding can lead to constant mental chatter and distraction, leaving you scattered and unfocused.

One of the most common excuses for not doing the things we want is a lack of time. This belief that there isn't enough time keeps us stuck in an energy of lack. When we believe this narrative, our feelings and actions align with what we don't have, in this case, time, instead of what we do want, which is more time. This mindset fosters self-doubt and resistance, zapping our motivation to pursue our goals. Consequently, we keep making excuses and finding evidence to support the notion that there's no time.

Holding ourselves responsible for the happiness and well-being of everyone else is a pretty heavy load, yet we do it anyway. When we develop this pattern of thinking and behavior, we make choices that don't serve us, like saying *yes* when we really want to say *no*. We end up feeling trapped, not knowing how to be any other way. We can even lose sight of our own identity, as I did when I gave all of my energy obsessing about my ex-boyfriend, sitting on my kitchen floor for hours, and scrolling social media to find out what girls he was talking to. At some point, we may even question our life purpose. *There's got to be more to life than this!*

Reclaim Your Time and Take Back Control

When I worked with Suzanne, it didn't make sense to start creating routines or working on new habits until we cleaned out the clutter of her daily life. The decluttering part of this process gave her the clarity she needed to start envisioning what her life could look like as an independent woman unapologetic for making decisions for her well-being. She saw herself with more freedom to indulge in healthy activities with friends, looking and feeling vibrant, and feeling happy, being in control of her time.

Without this step, it was like looking through foggy glasses. Once she had a vision, she could reframe her thinking to align with the version of herself she wanted to create and start focusing on the lifestyle modifications needed to get the results she wanted, which was to feel emotionally balanced, confident, and in control of her life again.

When Suzanne used the holistic health wheel to identify where she was most out of balance, she found that she needed to focus on her career, finances, and spirituality. After three months of using the time management system that I will share with you in a moment, her scores went from mid-level to high, and all areas of the health wheel were in harmony. Here's a snapshot of how she rated herself.

Areas of the Health Wheel	Before	After
Finances	5	8
Spirituality	5	9
Career	5	8
Nutrition	6	8
Movement	7	9
Connection	6	8
Sleep	9	9

Suzanne experienced a transformation after only three months. "Every part of me has grown, and I feel a lot more balanced in all of these areas. It's amazing how it's all connected. I feel like there's been a big shift."

There *was* a huge shift. At the time, Suzanne rated herself a five and six. She hadn't considered the interconnectedness of the different areas and how one area could offset the balance of the others. As soon as she was given a solution to get rid of the chaos and restore order, she was able to spend more time on her self-care, which improved her mood and reframed her mindset around her finances and teaching job. She scheduled time to prepare her meals and exercise, creating a habit of making healthier choices, and she leaned into her spirituality more deeply, which strengthened the connection she had with herself and others. In just three months, she regained her sense of self and embodied a higher version of who she used to be.

Self-Healing Invitation: Create Time Abundance

Here are some simple steps to help you create more time abundance and feel more relaxed with time. If you can stay consistent with the process each week, you will be well on your way to creating new habits that will put you back in control and give you the transformational improvements you desire.

Take a week to go through these steps. We're keeping this simple by only focusing on creating specific blocks of time for your three most important priorities. During this process, you will declutter and organize, get into alignment, and feel more at ease when it comes to your time.

I recommend that you revisit the holistic health wheel first and take a look at your results so you have a way to measure your progress before and after going through these steps. You may want to go through the exercise again anyway, depending on where you are at with your intentions since starting this book.

Where are you out of balance?

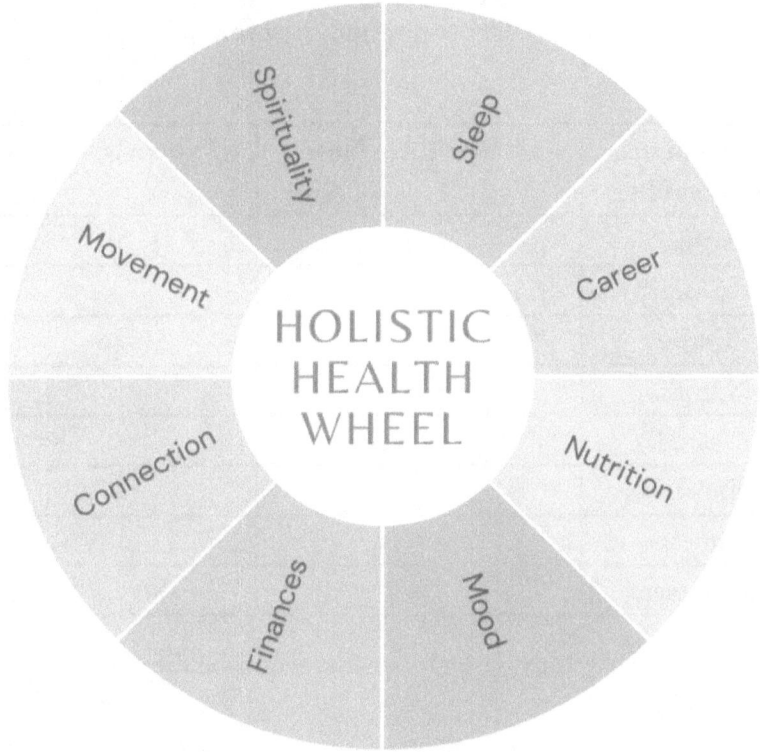

Instructions

1. Rate each area of health in the health wheel on a scale from 1-10, with 1 being the least satisfied and 10 being the most satisfied. Don't overthink it. What number immediately comes to mind? You'll receive the answers from your intuitive mind faster than your thinking mind, so write down the first number that pops into your head. Simply place your number in each piece of the pie.

2. Fill in the chart below with both your current ratings and the ratings of where you would like to be. Your rating can be the same for both columns. There are no right or wrong answers.

3. Answer the questions below the chart so you have a baseline.

Areas of the Health Wheel	Where I Am Now	Where I Want to Be
Spirituality		
Sleep		
Career		
Nutrition		
Mood		
Finances		
Connection		
Movement		

Where are the three largest gaps between where I am and where I want to be?

Where are there the smallest gaps?

Step One

Clear a week on your calendar

Whether you use a virtual or paper planner, take a moment to consider how and where you will use your calendar. Will you set it and forget it, or will you use it on the go and make it your daily navigational guide? Keep in mind that virtual calendars, like Google and Outlook, allow you to be more flexible in shifting and adjusting tasks as needed.

They can also synch between your phone and computer. Paper planners, on the other hand, make planning fun and can be a great creative outlet, using tools like colored pens and stickers. Use whatever feels good to you.

Step Two

Conduct a time audit

- Spend one full day keeping track of everything you do in a notebook or on your phone in Notes. Be as thorough as possible. Try to add the small stuff too, like making your coffee, driving to the store, engaging in conversation, or spending time on social media.
- Review your list at the end of the day and reflect on where you may have wasted some time. Did you spend too much time scrolling social media or watching television? Just notice. This exercise is simply about creating awareness of where some of your time is going.

Step Three

Dump and Declutter

- **Do a brain dump:** Set a timer for ten minutes and make a list of all of your to-do's. Don't leave anything out. It may look like a random list, but get everything on the paper. We tend to carry our to-do lists in our heads. We are going to write it all down and scrub the list.
- **Prioritizing:** On the same sheet of paper, write down your top three priorities for the week in a column to the right of your list. I recommend one of them aimed at your health.
- **Declutter:** First, circle everything on your list that absolutely must stay. Consider these your non-negotiables. Next look at your top three priorities and identify anything on your list that aligns with each priority. Draw a line connecting the task to the

priority. Anything left that doesn't line up with a priority for the week gets crossed off the list or tabled for another week.

Step Four

Organize

- **Create your time blocks:** Look at your priorities and create three time blocks to start. Give each block a name. I recommend using the areas of the holistic health wheel for your time block names to make it easy. The job of a time block is to organize all related tasks so your calendar doesn't function like a cluttered list of to-do items. Start with three that align with your top three priorities and build from there once you become comfortable with this exercise.
  - Example time blocks I use are:
    - **Focus time**—I use this for work that requires heavy concentration and no interruptions, such as my writing and creating.
    - **Appointments**—This includes medical, personal, or anything where a time has been agreed on to meet with someone else but can be changed if necessary.
    - **Fixed**—These are all of my non-negotiables where the day and time cannot change.
    - **Me time**—This is for any self-care routines like yoga, meditation, beach time, journaling, or naps.
    - **Group**—I use this for any meetings for personal programs I am in.
- **Give your time blocks a color:** Giving your time blocks a color will help you easily connect with the types of activities on your calendar. This quick snapshot can help you mentally prepare for the week ahead. For example, when I look at my week and see a lot of dark purple, I know right away that it's a heavy week for appointments. If I don't see much lavender, which is my *Me Time* block, I'll know I didn't schedule enough self-care. When I see red, I know I've remembered to carve out time for my errands.

Step Five

Drop in your time blocks

- Open your calendar to the week you cleared out for this exercise and drop in your non-negotiables first. For example, if you take your kids to school, that is not negotiable since it happens at the same time every day. Once you drop in all your non-negotiables for the week, you can start adding in your three time blocks.
- Keep your time blocks to under three hours unless it's a work shift. Even then, you can break up your work time block with some white space for intentional breaks to do some breathing, walking, stretching, or a short meditation.
- It's important to take breaks in between blocks and leave space to transition from one to another, avoiding burnout. Time blocks that overlap or run up right next to each other most likely mean you are running on autopilot.
- You have flexibility in how you organize your day. You can CHOOSE where to place your time blocks, and you can move them as needed throughout your week. The point is that they are on your schedule, and you have made a commitment to them.

Below is a look at my calendar. I added time blocks for things I know I want in my week first. I have plenty of white space for downtime or to schedule more activities, but I don't want to overcrowd my calendar. White space is a good thing! It means you are striking a balance between busy time and downtime.

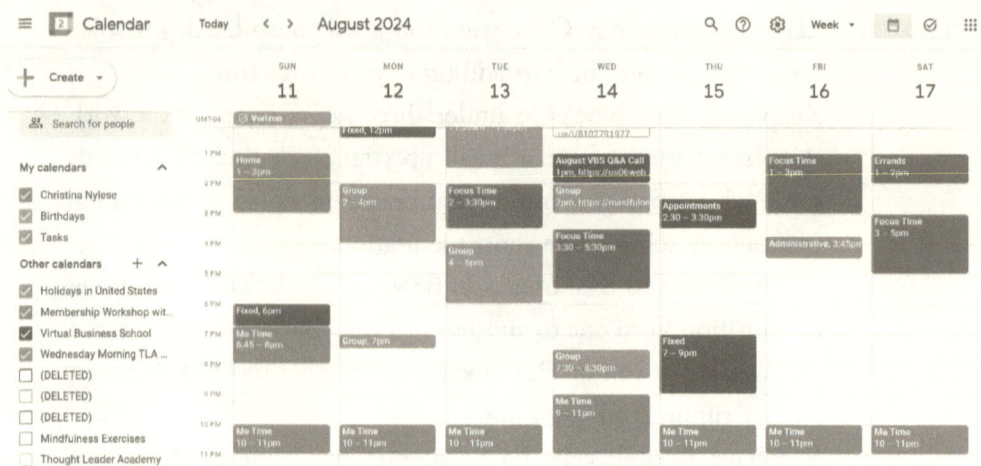

Once your time blocks are filled in for the week, open up each one and add your aligned tasks from your scrubbed list from Step Three into the notes section. Keeping your to-do items off the main page of the calendar keeps it neat and decluttered. Add only the ones that need to be on your schedule for this particular week. Remember, your time blocks contain your tasks, it isn't the task itself. For example, when I open up my *Errands* time block, you can see my tasks inside.

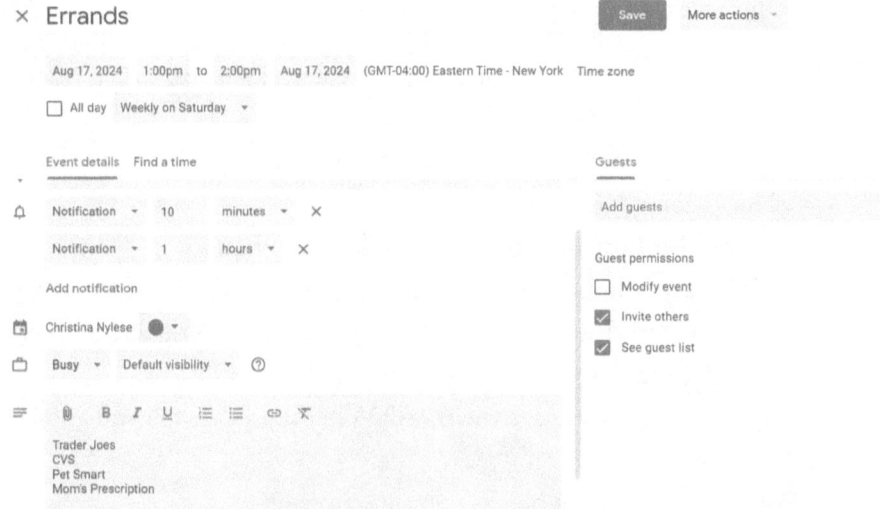

Time blocking might seem a bit uncomfortable at first if you're used to making lists and checking things off, but once you practice it, you'll be amazed at how quickly you start to feel more organized and in control. Keep your lists if it makes you feel accomplished to check things off. Just make sure those actions are also on your calendar. That way, you can make sure you are not over-tasking yourself, which will only leave you feeling overwhelmed. You will see in no time how in control you feel just by the way you set up your week.

Keep in mind that this process will take some trial and error until you adjust it to work for you. This is the foundational piece that you can now build upon. It starts you off feeling clean and organized with your time, making it easier and less stressful to incorporate the things you want to be doing more of. I am always adjusting my time blocks. In fact, I reassess my system with each season and make adjustments, so I always control my calendar instead of my calendar controlling me.

After you have completed your first round of this exercise, step back, look at your week, and ask yourself these questions:

1. Does my calendar represent my top three priorities?
2. Does my calendar look too crowded?
3. Do I have enough downtime or white space in between time blocks for rest and recharge?
4. Have I kept my time blocks to under three hours?
5. How easy will it be to move time blocks if needed?
6. How do I feel when I glance at my calendar? Do I feel at ease and in control, or anxious and overwhelmed?
7. What color do you see the most? What does that tell you about your schedule?
8. Are there any time blocks you can remove?

Take a look at your health wheel and your ratings. Do the time blocks and focused activities on your calendar align with where you want to be? Will they move the needle in helping you close the gaps? Are you setting yourself up to achieve the life balance you desire? The holistic health wheel is a great tool to use alongside this exercise each week to make sure you are aligned with your intentions.

As you practice this time management exercise each week, you will find it easier to build on your time blocks and add more. Just keep it simple at first, and you'll be feeling less stressed about time in no time! The Self-Healing Invitation gives you the opportunity to print out the exercise to use over and over again.

Download and print your Self-Healing Invitation here:

The time management system is a tool to help you prioritize your time so that you can focus on what matters the most to you. As you get better at this practice, you will become more aware of creating time not only for necessary daily actions but for personal time for vacations, family, fun, and adventure.

And that's where boundaries come in.

Chapter 13: Boundaries

If you're in a place of guilt, anger, and resentment, you need to check your boundaries.

When my client Suzanne and I began working together, she had already been going to a recovery program and a therapist. Her recovery program had been helping her to feel more spiritually connected, but she wasn't quite satisfied with the results she was getting in therapy. She wasn't even clear on what she needed to work on. She just knew how she wanted to feel, which was at peace, balanced, and in control of her life again. Her husband was in rehab for drinking, and she had spent two months doing nothing because she didn't know where to start. She was anxious because she felt like she was wasting time instead of working on herself. She had been learning to start taking responsibility for her part in things, but she'd still catch herself saying, "He did this to us. If he had only stayed sober the first three times, we wouldn't be here right now."

"There's nothing wrong with us. Life is pushing and hurting to get our attention. Sometimes the pain and pushing are pointing towards a lesson. The lesson may be that we've become too controlling. Or maybe, we're being pushed to own our power to take care of ourselves. The issue is boundaries." —
Melody Beattie, *The Language of Letting Go*

The most important kinds of boundaries are the ones we set for our own selves. If Suzanne wanted to feel at peace, emotionally balanced, and in control again, she would have to learn how to let go of her resentment and find a place in her heart for love and acceptance. Love and acceptance always start with us, and setting healthy boundaries can help.

Boundaries are the opposite of people-pleasing behaviors. They are an act of self-love, honoring your intentions and saying "yes" to yourself. However, old habits can be hard to change when trying to create new boundaries that support your well-being.

- You might feel guilty choosing yourself over others or **fear letting people down** if you say *no*.
- Perhaps you have a boss who constantly challenges your work, and you're **afraid to stand up for yourself** because you don't want to lose your job.
- Maybe **you don't know what you really want or need**, making it hard to recognize when you're pushing beyond your limits or sacrificing your personal well-being.
- Or maybe you have tried setting boundaries before, but people don't take them seriously, and **you feel disrespected**.

Whatever the reason, a lack of boundaries can leave you feeling angry, resentful, and frustrated. So, how do you know when your boundaries need some work? Here are some questions to consider:

1. Are you constantly feeling overwhelmed or stressed?
2. Do you find it challenging to say *no* to additional commitments?
3. Is there a balance between your personal and professional life?
4. Can you prioritize self-care without guilt?
5. Are there recurring situations where you feel your needs are not considered?
6. What does a lack of boundaries cost you?
7. What would change about your life if you set some healthy boundaries that allowed you time for yourself?

Even examining your calendar once you've implemented a time management system can be a good indication of how strong or weak your boundaries are. If you are still operating off a cluttered calendar or feel like you are doing so much but getting nothing done, it could have to do with your boundaries. Keep in mind that time blocking is a way of setting boundaries. If you are honoring your time blocks, you are honoring your boundaries.

Boundaries allow you to protect your physical and mental well-being by creating space for your self-care. Suzanne and I did this using the time management system so she could see for herself there was time for her to do what she wanted and a systematic way to make things happen consistently. When she sat down to create her calendar, it took away that feeling of overwhelm; she now knew how and when she could take care of herself the way she wanted. This empowered her to continue saying "yes" to herself and "no" to things that didn't align with her personal goals. She could just look at her calendar and feel more confident in her choices.

Suzanne had some concerns about falling back into old habits. She felt a lot stronger but still understandably shaky since sticking to her own boundaries was new for her. She was also unsure of how to respond if someone had a hard time accepting a boundary.

This is such a common concern, and the truth is that when we go through a transformation, this sometimes rattles the people closest to us. If you have never been good at setting boundaries with people, and all of a sudden, you're a boundary warrior, the people who used to cross lines with you may not like this change. It takes the power out of their hands and puts it into yours.

Feeling solid with your new boundaries requires two things:

1. *Know that their issue with your boundary is about them, not you.* If someone is going to be offended by or disrespectful of your boundary, that is their issue to resolve, not yours. The sooner you can be confident in that, the easier it will be to respond.
2. *Believe in yourself and your boundary.* Standing strong for your *no* takes the stress out of it for you. Be prepared with a response that you feel good about, one where you are clearly respecting yourself while being very clear with the other person. We don't

want to leave room here for a rebuttal. If you're ready with a response, you never feel thrown off guard.

Here are a few things you can say that could make setting boundaries easier. Keep your emotions out of it, and don't over-explain yourself. You don't owe anyone an explanation for your boundary. It's yours, and it's your birthright to have it. Practicing these responses can help build confidence and assertiveness over time.

Scenario 1: A colleague constantly asks you to help with their work.

Response: "I understand you're busy, but I have my own deadlines. Can we find another time to discuss this?"

Scenario 2: A neighbor shows up unannounced, and you're busy or in the middle of something and don't have time for a visit.

Response: "I appreciate you stopping by, but I'm in the middle of something and can't visit right now. Can we reschedule for another day?"

Scenario 3: You're out to dinner with a friend, and they are venting about their problems. It feels overwhelming, and it's consuming all of your time with her or him.

Response: "I'm sorry you're going through this, but I'm not in a place to help right now. Have you considered talking to a counselor?"

Scenario 4: You're asked to stay late at work but already have plans.

Response: "I have commitments I need to keep tonight. Can we discuss how to handle this tomorrow?"

Scenario 5: A friend frequently invites you to events you're not interested in.

Response: "Thank you for thinking of me, but I'm going to pass this time."

Then there is the short and sweet answer that always cuts to the chase: "No thanks."

Each of these responses shows either compassion or gratitude but also makes it clear you have responsibilities you need to make a priority. You are leaving an opening to discuss their request at another time, so it's not a complete shutdown.

Self-Healing Invitation: Boundary Audit

If you are still wobbly with your boundaries after trying out these responses, but you're determined to be a warrior boundary setter, here is a boundary audit you can try over the next 30 days: Choose one boundary you really want to land firmly with and consider some habits that will support that boundary. Maybe you need to set a boundary with your spouse and kids in the evenings to reserve some time for yourself to meditate, read, or take a hot bath. You might want to consider boundaries at work if you're not feeling respected and your boss is constantly adding more work to an already existing load. Consider one boundary and work on it for thirty days.

At the end of each week, reflect on your answers to the questions below so you know where you have made progress and where you still need to put in some work. Allow your progress to build on each week and assess where you are after the thirty days are up. Sometimes just holding ourselves accountable on paper where we can track our progress and cultivate awareness can provide the motivation and clarity needed to achieve our goals and make lasting changes.

Rate yourself on a scale from 1-10, with 1 being your needs were not met at all and 10 being your needs were completely met.

1. Were your physical, mental, and emotional needs met this week?
   1 = Not at all, 10 = Completely met

2. How much did certain activities, situations, or people drain your energy or cause stress?
   1 = Completely drained and stressed, 10 = No energy drained

3. How well did you set and honor limits or time blocks to support your boundaries?
   1 = Did not set any limits, 10 = Set and honored limits consistently

4. How consistent were you in practicing habits that support your boundaries?
   1 = Not consistent, 10 = Fully consistent

5. Do you feel the habits you've chosen to support your boundaries are effective?
   1 = Not effective, 10 = Extremely effective

6. How prepared are you to clarify your boundaries with others when necessary?
   1 = Not prepared, 10 = Fully prepared and confident

7. Did you communicate your boundaries with others effectively this week?
   1 = Not at all, 10 = Communicated clearly and confidently

8. How well was your boundary received by others?
   1 = Not well at all, 10 = Easily and respectfully

9. Did you surround yourself with people who respected your boundaries and well-being?
   1 = Not at all, 10 = Completely surrounded by supportive people

10. How effective was your boundary in supporting your well-being?
    1 = Not effective, 10 = Completely effective

11. Are you open to adjusting your boundaries to better align with your evolving needs?
    1 = Not open at all, 10 = Completely open to adjustments

Boundaries Audit Results Summary

81-110 (Strong Boundaries):

Overview: You understand your needs and limits, and you're effectively setting and communicating boundaries. Others likely respect your boundaries, and you maintain a healthy balance that supports your well-being.

Next Steps: Overall, you're doing an excellent job of protecting your time, energy, and personal needs. Continue to build on these strengths.

51-80 (Moderate Boundaries):

Overview: You're doing well in certain areas, but there may be inconsistencies. Some boundaries are respected, while others might need reinforcement or clearer communication. You may occasionally feel drained or overwhelmed, which is a sign that some boundaries aren't fully supporting you.

Next Steps: Focus on the areas where scores were lower and strengthen consistency, assertiveness in communication, or seeking support from others.

21-50 (Weak Boundaries):

Overview: Boundaries might be a challenge for you, leading to frequent overwhelm, exhaustion, or a sense that others aren't respecting your limits. It might feel challenging to firmly set boundaries.

Next Steps: Start small by identifying specific areas where you can set clearer boundaries. Practice saying "no" or allocating time for yourself without interruptions.

0-20 (Minimal or Absent Boundaries):

Overview: There is an urgent need to establish boundaries. You may often feel drained, taken advantage of, or lacking control over your time and energy. There's likely little distinction between your needs and what others ask of you.

Next Steps: Focus on the basics: identify a few personal needs and create boundaries that protect them. Practice communicating small boundaries with supportive people.

Once you've rated each question, take a moment to reflect on your scores.

What could you do to improve your boundary?

Are there specific actions or conversations that could help you strengthen this boundary?

How important is this boundary to you?

Download and print your Self-Healing Invitation here:

This provides an at-a-glance view of where your boundaries are working well and where they may need adjustment.

Setting boundaries is a skill that takes practice, just like time management. Using the time management practice from the previous chapter is a great first step if you are struggling with boundaries because your time blocks define the boundaries for you. Learning how to honor the time blocks is not only respecting yourself but also giving you the confidence to hold boundaries with others.

Be patient with yourself as you navigate this process and gradually become more comfortable with asserting and maintaining your boundaries. There will always be people who will resist them. Just remember, if you're feeling a little shaky, you can always revisit an earlier part of the book on mindset, your bully voice, nourishment, and connection to find something that is relevant to your particular struggle.

Now that we've learned how to reframe our thinking, nourish our minds and bodies holistically, and understand the importance of connection for our overall health, we can also see how setting boundaries around our time and relationships positions us to move forward. With these foundations in place, we are now ready to invite abundance into our lives in all its forms.

Chapter 14: Living Abundantly

I lost ten years of my life to drinking. From age twenty-nine to thirty-nine, drinking was my full-time job. I was either thinking about it or doing it, and because of that, I lived in a haze. I had no goals, passion, personal drive, or motivation, nor did I have the energy to make anything of my life. The high-achieving, responsible, and smart woman I was when I was younger was lost.

During my thirties, when I could have been planting roots, I watched my friends advance in their careers, get married, and start families while I isolated myself with a bottle of vodka.

Time kept moving, but I remained stuck, drowning in alcohol and completely unaware of the world around me.

This is why, when I got sober, time became very precious to me, and I didn't want to waste a minute. I was anxious to rebuild and move forward. But after years of chaos and unmanageability, I really needed to keep things simple and balanced. I had a lot of moving parts between living on my own again, getting my driver's license back, working my way up in a new career, and managing finances. It was a lot to handle on my own, and I knew if I tried to tackle everything at once, I'd lose my newfound sense of self and calm.

Back then, I didn't have the magical Google calendar that I use today, but I did use a paper planner. I had always been very systematic in the way I approached things. Even at a young age, I would plan my activities out on paper and move from one to the next in a timely manner. Systems were always how I operated, whether it was at home, school, or work.

The difference for me today is that I bring more intention to my time. I still follow my systems, but it's less about moving robotically from one thing to another and more about purpose. If I think about how I perceived time in the past, it looked like *how much can I get done in the time I have?* Today, it looks more like *what matters the most to me and what can I let go of to make more space for myself?*

I built my time management system with simplicity in mind. I've explored various trainings to hone my craft and continue to adjust it to work with the seasons of my life. Time has become one of my greatest assets, and when I use it intentionally, abundance in various forms shows up everywhere.

There is an undeniable connection between how we manage our time and the abundance of health, wealth, peace, and joy we experience. When I started coaching and shared my system with busy, high-achieving women who were overwhelmed and stressed, I heard the same feedback: they felt lighter, clear-headed, and more relaxed. They began clearing space for healthy routines like morning meditation, journaling, evening walks, or time to just breathe. Their days flowed with ease, and their focus shifted from taking care of everyone else to their own well-being. One client shared that after only two days, she woke up with a clear head for the first time in years. With this clarity of mind, she knew exactly how to approach her day, which made her feel in control and calm and helped her remain focused on the most important tasks. As her journey continued, she spent more quality time with her family, friends, and herself.

If you had asked me a few years ago what abundance means, I would have told you it was about financial success or material wealth. I thought abundance meant luxury—a big house, a fat bank account, or an overflow of things. But I know now that abundance is so much more than that. It's about having a life filled with what means the most to you. Abundance is what you define it to be, whether it be financial, health, friendships, travel, or happiness, and it can be found when we create the space to let it in.

Even when I left my job in 2023 to coach full-time, I believed my success would be measured by how well I did financially in my business. If I could replace my income in the first year, I'd consider myself "making it." I imagined financial abundance making it possible to renovate my condo, go on vacations, or maybe buy a summer home in Nantucket one day. That vision of material success filled me with excitement, but I didn't consider the abundance I already had, which was the energy that would ultimately fuel my path to the financial abundance I so badly wanted.

I ignored the blessings that were right in front of me, convinced they were distractions. I held off on dating until I'd made enough money in my business and could consider myself financially independent. I put off time with friends and family until the book was written. I consumed myself with online trainings I didn't need when I could have been out networking and collaborating with women who would help my business grow. What I wasn't seeing was that I needed the connections, the fun, the friendships, and love to fuel me. By cutting out these sources of joy, I was actually slowing down my path to financial success.

I remember a session with my therapist when she asked me a question that really struck a nerve. She asked, "What do you do for fun, Christina?" I paused for a good minute, staring at her like a deer in headlights. I couldn't give her an answer. Not only was I feeling alone, depressed, and defeated from my unstable romantic entanglement at the time, but I didn't have fun doing anything, nor did I intentionally make time for it. I could tell her about all the fun I had as a drinker, going out with friends to the bars, dancing on tables, and flirting with guys. I remembered the football games with beers and hosting dinner parties just so I could make fancy drinks for my friends. Even cleaning my house was fun if I was drinking. I drank to make things more fun because I didn't know how to create it or feel it on my own.

I was a good few years into recovery when she asked me this question. It became painfully clear to me that the joy and fun I once felt was wrapped up in the haze of drinking, and without it, I was lost, unsure of how to find joy in sobriety.

After that conversation, I did seek ways to bring more fun into my life, but as my life got busier and responsibilities weighed more heavily, fun was the first thing to go on the back burner. Plus, I was still so consumed with the messy, non-committed relationship I was in that I left no time for anything else, including things that would support my well-being.

The value of the time management system is to see for yourself how much opportunity for abundance you can create. Living abundantly is believing in life's possibilities and being open to receiving them. But we have to take inspired action. If I want to have more conversations and make more connections, then I need to clear space on my calendar to make that happen, or I'm basically putting a message out to the Universe that I don't have time for conversations. If I want a loving companion to come into my life, my calendar should reflect that by having space to invite it in.

Since that time with my therapist, I began a healing journey to bring harmony and balance into my life using the mindfulness, nourishment, and connection practices I've shared throughout this book. Once I learned how to detach using the 3-step process I shared in Chapter 10 and rewired my brain with more positive self-talk, I naturally sought ways to enhance my well-being. Quieting my bully voice about the relationship I was in gave me a renewed sense of self-respect. As I focused less on him and more on myself, I made rest, balanced nutrition, and friendships a priority. I started exploring natural health and holistic wellness as a career path. I started writing again. I smiled more. My zest for life returned, and as my health improved physically, emotionally, and spiritually, I was able to look back and see how off-balance the other areas of my health had been. I again found myself eager to not waste another minute of time giving my focus, attention, and energy to anyone or anything that did not serve my higher purpose.

My transformational lifestyle over the years has invited health, wealth, joy, and friendships back into my life. With these powerful sources of energy, things flow to me much more easily. When I feel like I am pushing hard to get something, the flow stops. When I let go and let it be, with the belief that there is enough abundance to go around, amazing things happen.

If you have been flowing with this book and practicing the exercises, you have likely already noticed a shift within yourself. Now that you know where it all leads, let's take a minute to reflect on the abundance we are creating in our lives.

Self-Healing Invitation: Abundance

Assess Your Abundance Mindset

- What do you need to believe to bring more abundance into your life?
- What energy do you need to be in to bring in this abundance?
- How often do you focus on what's lacking rather than what you already have?
- In what areas of your life do you feel a sense of abundance already (e.g., relationships, health, time, money)?

Create Your Abundance Journal

Over the next seven days, dedicate five minutes each evening to journal about the abundance in your life. Use the following prompts:

- Today, I noticed abundance in my life when _____
- I allowed abundance into my life today by _____.
- One thing I did to create more abundance today was _____.

Simple Exercises That Create an Energy of Abundance

Here are some simple and fun ideas that can help you cultivate a joyful mindset and abundant energy that will inspire new ideas for your rich, full, and juicy life.

1. Start a positivity jar.

Fill a jar with one positive thought or idea a day. At the end of the month, read them back to yourself and sit in gratitude with them. Recall why you wrote them down. Set an intention to practice living in this way. Come back to this practice when you need to uplevel your vibe.

2. Tap into your senses.

Pay attention to your senses with the small stuff, like the smell when you walk into a bakery, the sight of a flower blooming at the first sign of spring, the sounds of children laughing, the feel of your pet's soft fur, or the smell of soap when washing your hands. Be open to the opportunity for these small joys to fill your heart and soul.

3. Visualize

Thoughts turn to things. So, when you're not happy in your current situation, just sit with your eyes closed and visualize where you want to be. Create a delicious scene, and let the dream just go where it may. When you focus your thoughts on what you desire, again and again, you are creating your reality. Keep your thoughts on this happy person, place, or thing, and watch a version of it come into your life. Feel the joy of having it already. Then anticipate its arrival because it's already here for you.

4. Connect

Connect with loved ones regularly or reach out to friends with whom you can have meaningful conversations that are inspiring, uplifting, and insightful. Feeling connected to others fosters a sense of belonging and community, which contributes to a deeper sense of joy and fulfillment.

5. Get creative

Get creative with a do-it-yourself craft project. Whether it's painting, knitting, or making homemade candles, channeling your creativity into a hands-on project can be fun and fulfilling and give you a feeling of accomplishment.

6. Volunteer

Choose a local charity that speaks to your heart and dedicate some time to volunteer. Whether it's serving meals at a soup kitchen, walking dogs at a local animal shelter, or tutoring students, giving back to your community can bring a sense of purpose and joy.

7. Cook or bake

Spend an afternoon experimenting in the kitchen and trying out new recipes. Have fun browsing your favorite cookbooks or searching on Pinterest. Cooking or baking can be a therapeutic and rewarding activity, and you get to enjoy the fruits of your labor afterward.

8. Venture outdoors

Hiking, biking, camping, or kayaking are all activities where you can be outdoors and explore new territories. Challenge yourself to engage in a new activity you've never tried, making sure it is safe, and don't forget to bring supplies like water, trail mix, and sunscreen. New adventures outside can feel both liberating and exciting while getting a dose of Vitamin D and some serious emotional grounding.

9. Have a picnic

Pack a lunch or dinner spread, grab your family, friends, or just yourself, and head to your local park. Just enjoy being outdoors in the fresh air, sunshine, and the simple pleasure of dining outdoors.

10. Create a vision board.

Cut out pictures or words from magazines that represent how you want to feel and what you want your future life to look like. Write your own future bio. Put it on a corkboard and focus on it every day for at least a few minutes. Close your eyes and feel it real. Get excited. Make it your reality by telling yourself, "I claim this for myself. Therefore, it is done."

Download and print your Self-Healing Invitation here:

Afterword

Healing never ends. Just in writing this book, I went on a whole new healing journey I didn't expect. As stories long forgotten emerged, I felt a range of emotions, like grief, shame, anger, happiness, gratitude, love, and peace. I didn't plan on sharing many of the stories here. In fact, my plan was to share my experience, strength, and hope as a recovering alcoholic to illustrate how the mind and body can heal us from traumatic experiences. When I sat down to write, these stories about my other addictions just flowed out of me, as if I was being called to share them with the world, no matter how insignificant they seemed to me at the time. Reading it now, I recognize that what may seem trivial to me is quite significant to someone else and could have the power to influence someone to make a better choice and change their life forever.

I hope you leave this book with a fresh perspective on how our mind and body can heal us in the worst of times if we just give them half a chance. So often, we run to a doctor for the answers or a quick fix. I am not against doctors, but I am for an integrative approach to healing, whether it be emotional, physical, spiritual, or all three. On my unique path, I found how the powers of mindfulness, nourishment, and connection, which are now the pillars I use when empowering others, can heal us from the inside out. The mind is the most powerful tool we have, yet we often forget to use it.

It is with humble gratitude and deep affection for you, my reader, for picking up this book and going on this journey, whether it was from beginning to end or pieces here and there. My hope is that part, if not all, resonates with you and inspires you to have the courage to change what you CAN change so that you can break free from the cycle of addiction and move forward in health, peace, and freedom.

God, grant me the serenity to accept the things I cannot change, the courage to change the things I can, and the wisdom to know the difference.

Acknowledgments

When I started writing this book, I had a completely different plan for what I was creating. Thank you to my God, who had something else in mind for me, and for the spiritual guidance to listen to my intuition.

Thank you to my mom for never forgetting my journey and always being my number one fan and supporter.

Thank you to my dad in heaven for making the writing of this book possible and for always standing behind my love for writing. I know you are looking down proudly.

To my coaches and circles of women who played a significant role in my growth as I wrote this book. Your wisdom and guidance are unprecedented.

A huge thank you to Sara Connell and team at Thought Leader Academy for showing me what's possible and opening up space for me to bring my Big C Energy.

To my writing coach, Hannah, for pushing me ever so gently to go deep and give you more of myself throughout this book. It was so worth it.

To Claudine Mansour. You captured what was in my heart on the cover, and I am forever grateful.

A huge shout out and thank you to Jane Ubell-Meyer and team at Thought Leader Academy Publishing for making my first publishing experience so smooth and easy! Your guidance, thoughtfulness and generous support took all the first-time jitters away.

About the Author

Christina Nylese is a holistic health and recovery coach dedicated to helping men and women break free from their self-sabotaging behaviors and addictive patterns, and reclaim control over their lives—whether they're navigating recovery or simply seeking a more empowered existence. With over thirteen years of sobriety and personal healing, Christina brings a deep understanding of what it takes to overcome life's biggest obstacles.

Her holistic approach and unique perspectives have empowered countless men and women to shed old habits, manage stress, and build lives filled with purpose and abundance.

Known for her relatable guidance and unwavering support, Christina's work goes beyond coaching—she equips her clients with mindfulness and self-care tools to thrive, fostering transformations that last. Through her programs and one-on-one work, she has helped people from all phases of life regain their confidence, reclaim their power, and live in alignment with their goals and values.

Based in Naples, Florida, Christina finds her own balance through running, spending time in nature, fierce self-care, and playing with her cat, Lucy. Her most cherished moments are spent with her mom, who has Alzheimer's and has been her greatest example of what it truly means to live in the moment.

www.ingramcontent.com/pod-product-compliance
Lightning Source LLC
Chambersburg PA
CBHW021149130626
46554CB00005B/1731